Treago Castle from the South-West.

THE CASTLES OF HEREFORDSHIRE AND WORCESTERSHIRE

CONTENTS

INTRODUCTION TO THE CASTLES OF HEREFORDSHIRE

MOTTE AND BAILEY CASTLES

Before the Normans arrived in England in the mid 11th century all fortifications in what had by then become the county of Hereford were built by communities or the state. The concept of privately owned defensible residences does not appear to have been known or favoured among the Saxons. In 1049 the defeat of Bishop Ealdred of Worcester by Gruffydd ap Rhydderch of South Wales prompted Ralph of Mantes and his neighbours to build castles at Hereford, Ewyas Harold, and Richard's Castle. Ralph, a nephew of King Edward the Confessor, was a Norman, and the castles were regarded as novel and alien to English culture. Their existence caused friction at King Edward's court between his Norman friends and the Anglo-Danish party led by Earl Godwin. The castle at Ewyas was destroyed in 1052 after Godwin and his sons returned from a brief period of exile, and when the Welsh sacked Hereford in 1055 it would appear that Godwin's son Harold, then holding the reins of government, concentrated on the refortification of the city rather than rebuilding the castle.

In 1067 the newly crowned William I (The Conqueror) granted the earldom of Hereford to his cousin William Fitz-Osbern, described as the ablest officer and bravest Norman in his army. He was thus granted an unusually compact group of estates with special powers to rule Herefordshire as one of a series of semi-independent areas forming a buffer zone between the newly conquered English and the then unconquered Welsh. William Fitz-Osbern and other lords such as Roger de Lacy and Hugh de Mortimer, and their knights, formed a thin veneer of landowning, French speaking, Normans in a district populated by Saxons and vulnerable to Welsh attacks. They rapidly consolidated their uneasy hold on Herefordshire by filling it with castles built with the aid of slave labour. In the four years prior to being killed in Normandy in February 1071 William Fitz-Osbern alone rebuilt the castles of Ewyas Harold and Hereford, and built new ones at Clifford and Wigmore, thus three more in Monmouthshire.

On a rocky site, which was unsuited to the digging of great earthworks, at Chepstow in Monmouthshire William Fitz-Osbern built a stone keep containing a hall above a low basement, but all the early castles in Herefordshire were not built of stone, but of earth and wood. These were quicker, easier, and cheaper materials to work with, especially as there was a comparative lack of stone masons. The usual form comprised an earthen mound or motte surmounted by a timber tower with a small palisaded court around it, and at the base was a bailey, or larger court, surrounded by a rampart and ditch and a palisade, and containing a hall, chapel, workshops, stables, granary, and sundry farmyard buildings, all of wood. The tower on the mound formed a private dwelling for the lord and a last refuge should the weaker bailey defences succumb to an attack. The basic design varied according to the terrain and the labour and time available. A small enclosure with high banks (known to castle enthusiasts as a ringwork) was sometimes provided instead of a motte, and baileys were omitted or duplicated and made whatever shape and size local circumstances dictated. Natural landscape features were utilised whenever possible, hillocks and spurs being shaped and heightened into steep-sided, level-topped mottes. The Welsh Border counties contain the highest concentration of motte and bailey castles in Britain, and there are over 90 of them in Herefordshire. Good examples are Ewyas Harold, Clifford, Richard's Castle, Snodhill, Dorstone, and Wigmore.

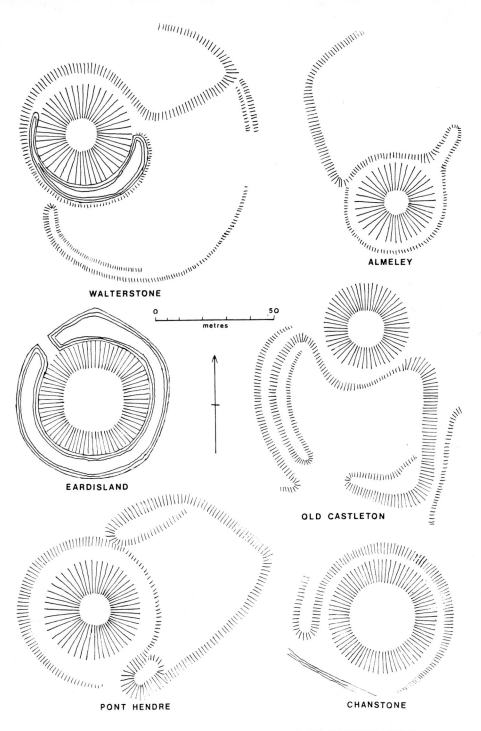

WALTERSTONE

ALMELEY

EARDISLAND

0   50
metres

OLD CASTLETON

PONT HENDRE

CHANSTONE

PLANS OF MOTTE & BAILEY CASTLES IN HEREFORDSHIRE

3

Almeley Motte

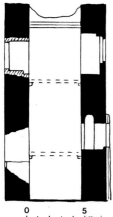

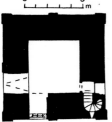

PLAN & SECTION OF
GOODRICH CASTLE KEEP

STONE CASTLES

Timber is vulnerable to accidental or deliberate destruction by fire, and soon rots away when in constant contact with the soil. Gradually, at the most important castles the timber portions were replaced with mortared stone. There is no evidence to suggest any Herefordshire castle possessed any stone defences prior to King Stephen's reign. At Goodrich is a small square tower keep of c1150-70 containing a basement, a lofty hall above, and a bedroom on top. On the motte at Richard's Castle is the lower part of a late 12th century octagonal tower keep, and parts of the gateway there may be also of that era. Hereford Castle appears to have had a large rectangular tower keep and stone walls around the bailey by the end of the 12th century, but nothing remains of them, whilst whatever 12th century stone walls existed at Wigmore were mostly rebuilt in the early 14th century. The fragments of an enclosing wall around the summit of the big mound at Kilpeck (termed by modern writers a shell keep) are thought to be late 12th century. Another shell keep stood at Wigmore, and foundations of another, much smaller in size, remain at Llancillo. There is also evidence to suggest that small square stone towers once stood on the mounds at Downton and Bredwardine.

4

The 13th century is the most notable period for stone castles in Herefordshire. Of c1200-20 are the rather unusual shaped keep at Snodhill, which probably just contained a single living room set over a basement, and the hall-block with a tall round tower at one corner set within a rectangular moated site at Pembridge. The tower is regarded by many writers as a keep, although it is much smaller than others of that type. The large three storey round tower keep and bailey walls at Longtown are now regarded as the work of Walter de Lacy in c1216-23 when he was sheriff of the county and its most eminent baron. Lyonshall has the base of another round tower keep built in the 1220s by one of de Lacy's knights, whilst a third is thought to have been built by the de Braose family in c1216-25 on the mound at Huntington, and a fourth to have been built at Moccas in the 1290s.

A small rectangular stone walled court was built at Goodrich in c1220-45, and in the same period small polygonal courts were built on the mound summits at Hereford, Clifford, and Ewyas Harold. In each case there were round flanking towers, and these were also provided in the slightly larger enclosure of this period at Weobley, where there was also a large rectangular keep with round corner towers, a plan favoured in Ireland rather than England in this era.

In the period c1270-1300 the curtain walls, turrets, and twin-towered gatehouse at Pembridge were built, and the old earthworks at Wilton were modified to take a rectamgular courtyard with round and polygonal flanking towers. In grandeur and massiveness but not overall scale, both are eclipsed by the splendid new works of the same era at Goodrich, producing a building of an advanced design which combined great defensive strength with stately apartments. The chambers are set around a small court and are constructed as integral units with new curtain walls. At one corner is a large gatehouse containing a chapel and other fine rooms, whilst further important chambers are contained within large round towers rising from square bases set on the other corners. Goodrich is now by far the most interesting and best preserved Herefordshire castle despite being very ruined, and is the only one where any medieval domestic apartments have survived in an understandable state.

The Mortimers' chief seat at Wigmore Castle as rebuilt in the early 14th century comprised a large bailey with various towers of mostly rectangular shape, with, towering over all, an oval shell keep with a tower house or range of apartments at one end. Other apartments appear to have been ranged around a rectangular middle court set on a shelf on one side of the mound. The outer bailey protecting two sides of the inner court at Goodrich is also of this period, whilst the towers added to the bailey wall at Snodhill may be of the 1360s.

Goodrich Castle: The Keep & SE Tower.

5

As times became more peaceful after Edward I's defeat of the Welsh in the 1280s there was less need for massive and very expensive fortifications. However, military features were often retained in the design of new buildings to give protection against any unruly neighbours or peasantry, and as status symbols indicating lordly rank. An early example of such a lightly fortified manor house was Ashperton Castle, for which a licence to crenellate ws granted in 1296. Only the moat now remains. Parts of the hall and rectangular gateway of an early 14th century mansion remain at Brampton Bryan. They occupied most of two ranges set either side of a narrow court. Other ranges with apartments and service rooms would have occupied the other two sides. There would have been a moat but probably no flanking towers, although later in the 14th century an outer portion with two round towers was added in front of the gateway. Little now remains of the contemporary castle at Penyard, but it is assumed to have had a similar layout.

Kentchurch Court

Kentchurch Court has a keep-like corner tower, hall range, and a gatehouse remaining from a late 14th century courtyard mansion, while Hampton Court has a large gatehouse and corner turrets, and was licensed in 1431. The castles of Bronsil, licensed in 1449 and 1460, Croft, probably of the 1470s, but possibly somewhat earlier, and Treago, which in its present form is of c1490-1500 onwards, all had corner towers, gatehouses, and four ranges of apartments set around central courts. None of them was of importance militarily, and moats formed the primary defensive measures.

Treago Castle from the south.

Scattered across Herefordshire, but more numerous in the east half of the county, where there are less mottes, are platforms with surrounding moats marking the sites of former manor houses, most of which were not otherwise fortified. In many cases the original internal buildings were of perishable materials. The half-timbered 14th century house and 15th century gatehouse at Brockhampton may have been typical of these structures. Excavation of the platform at Breinton, however, exposed the foundations of a 12th century stone hall house with a thin surrounding curtain wall. The site is thought to have served as the vicarage for about a century. Most of the moats date from the 13th and 14th centuries, the most common form being a water filled ditch about 10m wide and up to 3m deep surrounding a roughly rectangular platform from 40m to 60m long. The few moats such as that at Edwin Ralph with round platforms may represent an earlier type transitional from mottes with higher but usually smaller summits, and there are earthworks such as that at Dilwyn which could be classed either as a defensible ringwork or a purely domestic round moated site. However, few Herefordshire moats have been excavated and/or properly surveyed, so many details about their history and purpose can only be surmised.

The digging of ditches was not regulated like the construction of embattled walls, but as only the gentry and wealthier clerics could obtain the labour needed to create them, moats became status symbols. They were not necessarily defensive in a military sense. They would serve to keep out vagrants and wild animals, and keep in children, servants, and domestic animals. They were valued as scenic features, and also as habitats for fish, eels, and water fowl, which together formed a substantial part of the medieval diet.

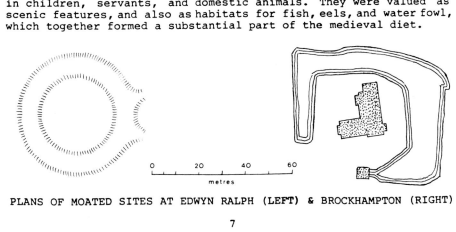

PLANS OF MOATED SITES AT EDWYN RALPH (LEFT) & BROCKHAMPTON (RIGHT)

THE MARCHER LORDS

King Stephen campaigned in Herefordshire in 1138 but the county was held throughout his reign by the supporters of his rival Empress Matilda. She, in 1141, created a new earldom of Hereford for Miles of Gloucester. Miles' son Roger, plus Hugh de Mortimer and Gilbert de Lacy were the chief Herefordshire barons when Henry II succeeded to the throne in 1154. Other families to come into prominence in the later 12th century were the de Bohuns, whom King John created Earls of Hereford in 1199, and the de Braose family, whose power was broken by John in 1208. With the demise of the main line of the de Lacys in 1241 the Mortimers and Bohuns remained the chief barons throughout the 13th and 14th centuries. They took opposing sides in the conflicts of the 1260s between Henry III and the barons led by Simon de Montfort, but both opposed Edward II (see page 46).

In the 15th century the Bohun estates passed to the Staffords, and the Mortimer lands passed to the Dukes of York, becoming their power base in the struggles against the house of Lancaster in the 1450s and 60s. Further details about these families and also those of Pembridge, Baskerville, Beauchamp, Devereux, Clifford, Chandos, Talbot, Verdon, Solaris, Grey, Harley, Say, plus others and some of the Bishops of Hereford, can be found in the gazetteer entries.

As a result of special powers having been granted to various barons in the Early Norman period in order to create centres of military power to keep the Welsh in check, most of the western parts of Herefordshire formed Marcher lordships. In these the royal officials had no power, their lords being answerable only directly to the Crown. They soon became an embarrassment and a danger to the King. Their lords insisted on independence when the Welsh were weak and divided, but cried out for royal support when the Welsh united behind one ruler and became dangerous. Although the Welsh defeat in the 1280s made the lordships anacronistic, they survived until abolished by Henry VIII in 1536. Wigmore, Lugharnes, Ewyas Lacy, Huntingdon, Eardisley, Whitney, Winforton, Clifford, and Ewyas Harold then became part of Herefordshire, whilst Michaelchurch and Radnor were lost to the new county of Radnor. Many of the medieval lordly families had died out or lost their main seats by then, and others such as the Cornewalls, Scudamores, and Coningsbys had risen to take their place as M.P.s, justices, and leaders of the militia.

Wilton Castle

In c1115 Henry I ordered that no private fortifications were to be constructed without his permission, and from the end of the 12th century onwards castle building had to be authorised by the Crown with a licence to crenellate, which was a sign of favour and trust. There are several licences which refer to buildings in the eastern part of Herefordshire but it does not appear that castle-building in the Marcher lordships was subject to this rule. On the contrary, in 1403 Henry IV specifically ordered all the castles in the lordships, some of which were decayed, to be refortified and held against the Welsh rebellion led by Owain Glyndwr.

THE POST-MEDIEVAL PERIOD

Castles were expensive to maintain and by the 14th century many of those built in the 12th and 13th centuries were becoming neglected. The Welsh rising under Owain Glyndwr was the principal occasion on which the military strength of Herefordshire castles was valued or tested between the conflicts of the 1260s and the Civil War of the 1640s, although there was also considerable unrest throughout the reigns of Edward II and Henry VI. By the 15th century many castles had passed into the hands of lords who had other more comfortable and less remote residences elsewhere. Henry VIII's topographer John Leland travelled through Herefordshire in c1535-40, and reported that many of the castles were decayed or totally ruined. By then Goodrich, Pembridge, Wilton, Eardisley, and Wigmore may have been the only older castles still regularly inhabited by those who owned them, or close relatives, although the more recent and often more comfortable fortified manor houses were all probably still in use. New domestic accommodation was built at Pembridge and Wilton in the 16th and 17th centuries, whilst the superior medieval chambers at Goodrich were evidently regarded as adequate without any notable alterations right up to the destruction of the castle.

When civil war broke out between King Charles I and Parliament in 1642 the Herefordshire gentry mostly supported Charles or stayed neutral. The chief exception was the Harleys of Brampton Bryan. Many castles were hastily patched up and garrisoned, but others, such as Wigmore, were wrecked to prevent the opposing side occupying them. The city of Hereford was occupied by Parliamentary troops for parts of 1642 and 1643, and was attacked by a Scottish army under the Earl of Leven in August 1645, but it was only after the city fell to a surprise attack by Colonel Birch in December 1645 that the King's cause in the county was lost. It was then just a matter of time before the many lesser Royalist garrisons submitted, the last being Goodrich Castle, which held out until the end of July 1646. During and after these sieges all the castles which were regarded as still tenable as fortresses were wrecked. Hereford Castle seems to have survived the wars intact only to be completely demolished a few years afterwards. Dismantled castles provided a convenient supply of stone for other building works throughout the 17th and 18th centuries, leaving little for us to study now.

The mansions of Hampton Court and Treago Castle, which were not capable of serious defence, appear to have survived the Civil War intact, and Croft Castle was soon repaired and re-occupied, only to be drastically remodelled in the 18th century. Kentchurch Court also survives in a habitable, although very altered, state. A house has been built into the ruins at Wilton, and Pembridge Castle was rebuilt in the late 17th century, and again earlier this century. All the other buildings are ruins or reduced to mere earthworks.

GAZETTEER OF CASTLES IN HEREFORDSHIRE

ALMELEY CASTLE
SO 332514

The churchyard has in recent years encroached upon the filled-in ditch of the NE side of the quadrangular bailey measuring about 50m across each way. On the south side is a motte rising about 8m high to a summit 11m in diameter. The castle would have been difficult to defend after the church was provided with a west tower in c1200. Although supposedly connected with Sir John Oldcastle, the Lollard executed by Henry V in 1417, the castle is most unlikely to have then still been in use. It is much more likely that Sir John lived at the 14th century manor house NW of the church.

ASHPERTON CASTLE
SO 642415

In 1292 Edward I licensed the Burgundian William de Grandison to crenellate his house here. It later passed to the Milburnes and the Monningtons. All remains of the buildings had vanished by the 18th century when the site was planted with trees. An oval platform 58m from north to south by 45m wide is surrounded by a wet moat which opens out almost to a square and is crossed by a causeway on the east. The church immediately to the east lies within a feintly deliniated rectangular outer enclosure.

ASHTON MOTTE & CASTLE
SO 514650 and 517642

North of the village is a mound 6m high on one side overlooking a stream, whilst SE of the village is the site of what is thought to have been a later medieval fortified house. It has a platform 3m high with upon it a rectangular mound 1m high and 30m square, and a round mound 14m in diameter and 1m high.

ASTON MOTTES
SO 462719 and 462721

NE of the church is a mound rising 7m to a summit 21m in diameter. About 200m to the north is a second mound 3m high with traces of what appears to be a small bailey platform to the west.

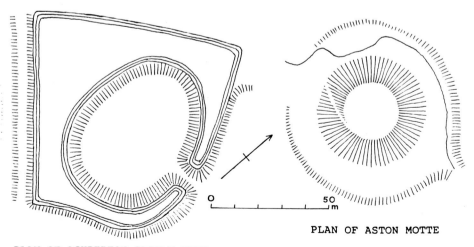

PLAN OF ASTON MOTTE

PLAN OF ASHPERTON CASTLE SITE

10

BRAMPTON BRYAN CASTLE

In the reign of Henry I Bernard Unspec, Lord of Kinlet in Salop, took the surname de Brampton from the estate he held here from the Mortimers in return for castle-guard service at Wigmore. The site is of strategic importance, there being traces of a Roman fortlet nearby, and it is assumed that Bernard erected a castle here. There was certainly a tower (perhaps of wood) and curtilage here in 1293 when a survey of Bryan de Brampton's estates was made after his death. The property passed to Robert Harley, who built a mansion on the earlier earthworks with a hall and gatehouse set either side of a narrow court, and presumably further ranges on the other two sides. A wide wet moat would have been the chief defensive feature. The imposing outer part of the gatehouse with round towers set on either side of the outer portal is thought to have been added later in the 14th century by Bryan de Harley, probably in imitation of the outer gateway at Clifford Castle. Thus strengthened militarily the mansion was held against Owain Glyndwr and the Welsh in 1403.

In the spring of 1642 Sir Robert Harley fortified the mansion for Parliament, leaving his wife Brilliana in charge whilst he was away in London. The surrounding district was then controlled by the Royalists, and in July 1643 Sir William Vavasour, governor of the city of Hereford, laid siege to the house. Lady Harley and about 100 men put up a brave defence until the Royalists withdrew their remaining forces from the blockade in September, Vavasour and some of his men having already gone off to help King Charles lay siege to Gloucester. Lady Harley died from the stresses of the siege not long afterwards, and it was the family doctor Nathan Wright who commanded the 60 or so men that vigorously resisted attacks by Sir Michael Woodhouse for three weeks until the house was surrendered in April 1644. The walls are said to have been battered down to the ground, leaving only cellars, but this is clearly something of an exaggeration. In 1661 a new mansion was constructed alongside by Sir Edward Harley, but the chambers above the inner gateway of the old house remained in use until damaged by a storm in the mid 18th century. The ruins now serve as a garden ornament to the new house.

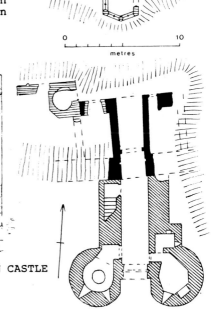

0   10
metres

BRAMPTON BRYAN CASTLE

11

Only the south wall remains of the 14th century hall range. It contains the entrance doorway, now covered by a late 16th century porch, which led into the screens passage at the east end of the room, which was probably about 7m wide. Set on either side of the doorway are contemporary loops, the eastern of which lighted the solar or a room below it. The original gatehouse was a three storey building lying only 9m south of the hall across what was probably once a cobbled court. It measured about 9.2m by 5.4m externally and had guard rooms set either side of a passageway about 2m wide and two large and pleasant rooms above. The north wall still survives almost to the full height and has two windows and a fireplace of the room over the passageway, and a top storey window, but the end walls of the building have gone, and little remains of the thicker south wall. The staircase turret adjoining the NW corner was added in the late 16th century when the adjoining apartments were rebuilt.

The late 14th century barbican or outer part of the gatehouse more than doubled the length of the entrance passage and closed it with a second portcullis. In one side is a straight mural stair to the upper storey rooms, and on the other is a projection containing a latrine. The round towers each have an exterior diameter of 4.6m and contain round and polygonal rooms with narrow loops and single light windows. Both towers partially retain their battlements. The earthworks of the castle have been dramatically changed since the Civil War, much of the platform about 3m high on which the central court lay having been cut away and the moats completely filled in.

Bronsil Castle.

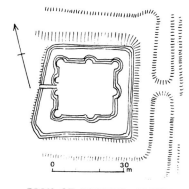

PLAN OF BRONSIL CASTLE

0   30
         m

BREDWARDINE CASTLE

SO 335444 and 336440

The earthworks and buried foundations lying beside the River Wye immediately south of the church are now regarded as relics of the mansion built by Roger Vaughan in c1640. It later passed to the Cornewall family and was dismantled, stone from it being taken to Moccas Court in 1775-81. It would appear that in the 12th century a stronghold stood on the mound in woodlands to the south, beyond the fishponds. Excavations here revealed traces of wooden buildings and the base of a small square stone tower. This site may be the old castle mentioned in the 13th century.

Bredwardine was held by John de Bredwardine in the late 11th century. The castle was probably built by the Baskervilles, who certainly held it in 1227, although the manor was held by their overlords the Bohun Earls of Hereford. There is no mention of a castle in an estate inventory of 1374 at about which time the lands passed by marriage to the Fouleshurst family of Cheshire, and in 1439 when William Fouleshurst died and Bredwardine passed back to the Baskervilles, there was another survey describing the site as waste and of no value. The Baskerville of that time, Sir John, lived at Eardisley Castle rather than in any house at Bredwardine.

BREINTON MOAT

SO 473395

Excavations at the rectangular moated enclosure SW of the church revealed the footings of a two storey hall block with a latrine turret at the SE corner, and of thin curtain walling on the inner edge of the moat. The site was only in use from the 12th century to the early 13th, and is thought to have been the early vicarage.

BRONSIL CASTLE

SO 749372

Richard, Lord Beauchamp of Powick, High Treasurer to Henry VI was licensed in 1449 and 1460 to crenellate his manor house at Bronsil. When his son Richard, 2nd Lord Beauchamp, died in 1496 it passed by marriage to the Rede family of Lugwardine. The building was burnt during the Civil War and although most of the outer walls remained standing in 1731, when the Buck brothers made an engraving of the ruins, only one corner tower still stood by 1779.

The site comprises a platform about 50m square, now overgrown with bushes and trees, and surrounded by a wide wet moat with a slightly irregular layout on the west. On this side is a bridge to a gateway which was flanked by polygonal towers with an exterior diameter of about 4.5m with walling about 1m thick. The outer part of the northern tower still remains and slight traces of footings are visible elsewhere on the site. There were other towers set at the corners and the middle of the other three sides. The hall must have been in the east range with apartments and service rooms set along the north and south ranges.

CASTLE FROME

SO 671458

On a strong tree-clad site at the end of a ridge high above the church is a motte about 4m high and a bailey. Castle Frome is mentioned several times in the 13th century and in 1242-3 was held by Gilbert de Lacy of Cressage, one of a minor branch of the family.

Clifford Castle: The Hall Block.

CLIFFORD CASTLE

SO 243457

It would appear that the castle founded by William Fitz-Osbern in c1069-70 was at Old Castleton, and the settlement which had some 16 burgesses at the time of Domesday may also have been there. By that time Clifford was held by Ralph de Todeni. His daughter and heiress Margaret married Richard Fitz-Pons, and either he or their son Walter, who took the surname de Clifford, must have raised the earthworks of the present castle. Walter's daughter Rosamund, famed for her beauty, and as the mistress of Henry II, was probably born at Clifford, although the family had a number of estates elsewhere.

It was the third Walter de Clifford, who succeeded in 1221 and lived until 1263, who replaced the original timber buildings with stone structures. It is likely that they were mostly complete by 1233 when Henry III ordered Walter to pay off the large debts that he owed the Jews, no doubt as a result of the expense of the new works. Walter had the royal messenger "eate the King's Writ, waxe and all", and the incensed King captured Clifford Castle in August of that year. Robert Clifford, the great grandson of Walter III's cousin Roger, was created Lord of Westmorland in 1310, and from then until the line became extinct in 1675 the chief family seat was at Skipton Castle in Yorkshire.

Matilda, heiress of the third Walter Clifford, was abducted by John Giffard of Brimsford, and by marrying her he legally obtained Clifford Castle. Their daughter and heiress married Henry de Lacy, Earl of Lincoln, on whose death in 1311 Clifford passed to the Mortimers of Wigmore. The Mortimers entertained Richard II and John of Gaunt at Clifford Castle in 1381, and garrisoned it against the Welsh in 1403. However Sir Edmund Mortimer was then Owain Glyndwr's prisoner at Harlech and forced to change sides, and Henry IV gave Clifford and Glasbury in 1404 to Sir Robert Whitney in gratitude for the services of his father as sheriff of Herefordshire. The castle was subsequently little used and fell into decay. In 1547 Clifford was granted to Lord Clinton, but his heirs appear to have sold it not long afterwards. It was later held by the Wardours.

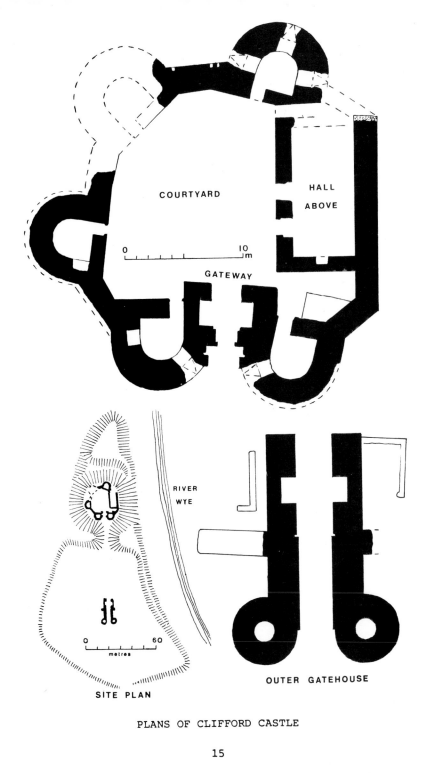

COURTYARD

HALL ABOVE

0   10 m

GATEWAY

RIVER WYE

SITE PLAN

OUTER GATEHOUSE

0   60
metres

PLANS OF CLIFFORD CASTLE

15

Clifford Castle: One of the tower bases.

The castle consists of a substantial mound lying high above the south bank of the River Wye, with a small triangular platform, now hopelessly overgrown, to the west, and a much larger, lower, and less well defended enclosure to the east. On the mound summit are ruins of a D-shaped enclosure measuring about 20m across within a wall about 2m thick, the straightest side being that facing the river. Abutting against this wall is a block of apartments which contained a hall about 12.5m long by 5.4m wide with windows looking out over the river. Below were two rooms which were probably dark and only used for storage or as accommodation for lesser mortals. On the east side of the court is a gateway passage with a portcullis groove and on either side a D-shaped tower about 3.5m in diameter inside walls about 2m thick. These towers are reduced down to about chest height, and even less remains of two others on the southern side, but a westward facing tower still stands high. It has a room at courtyard level with three embrasures for shooting slits, while above was a room with larger openings to both the field and to the court, and a passage to latrines set in the thickness of the wall to the south. There are no other signs of chambers within the court, and the hall block, plus three rooms in each of the towers, and perhaps rooms set between the hall block and the northern gateway tower evidently provided all the necessary accomodation.

The west platform shows no sign of stone buildings. A mound in the middle of the large east enclosure was excavated in 1951-4 by Air Commodore Douglas Iron, and found to contain the lower portion of a substantial gatehouse 8m wide by 16m long with turrets 5.7m in diameter projecting from the eastern corners. The turrets were solid at ground level but contained tiny round rooms higher up. The passageway was closed by a portcullis halfway along its length and has two short recesses in the side walls of the inner section. Two short lengths of curtain walling 2m thick adjoin the sidewalls but there are no other remains of the bailey wall. It was either never completed or had been thoroughly destroyed. In 1657 tne chancel of the castle chapel was still standing in the eastern, unwalled, part of the bailey. The nearby cottage may be built from its materials.

CROFT CASTLE

Domesday Book records Bernard de Croft as holding Croft, Wharton, and Newton from William de Schoies. The Crofts appear to have had a fortified house on this site throughout the medieval period and parts of the outer walls and the four round corner towers of the existing building go back to at least the 15th century, and perhaps the late 14th. Leland records the house as being "sett on the browe of a hill, somewhat rokky, dychid and waulled castle like". The Crofts were almost continuously represented in Parliament from 1296 until 1727, and were often sheriffs of Herefordshire. They were closely linked with the Mortimers of Wigmore. Sir Richard Croft held important positions in Edward IV's household, and under Henry VII became Treasurer, and a Privy Councillor. He was also Steward to Prince Arthur at Ludlow. Although temporarily disgraced during Queen Mary's reign, his great grandson Sir James Croft, who died in 1590, held various appointments under Edward VI and Elizabeth I. It was probably he who rebuilt the north side of the castle and planted the avenues of oak and chestnut trees in the grounds. His grandson Sir Herbert Croft, and his kinsmen the Scudamores, Wigmores, and Warnecombes, had a feud with Thomas Coningsby of Hampton Court in the 1580s which amounted almost to a private war. Subsequently he embraced the Catholic faith and died in 1629 as a monk at Douai in Flanders. His son Sir William Croft was a Royalist who fared badly in the Civil War. According to a Parliamentary news sheet Croft Castle was plundered by Irish levies to whom the Royalists owed pay, and shortly afterwards the castle was slighted by the Royalists to prevent Parliament occupying it, whilst Sir William was killed in June 1645 after a skirmish at Stokesay. In 1671 Sir Herbert Croft, son of Dr Herbert Croft, Bishop of Hereford, was made a baronet. His son Sir Arthur Croft got into debt, and Croft Castle was transferred to Richard Knight of Downton in 1746. His son-in-law Thomas Johnes built the present entrance in the east range, probably on the site of a gatehouse demolished in the Civil War. The second Thomas Johnes disposed of Croft to Somerset Davies of Wigmore, who was living in the castle in 1785, and in 1923 his descendants, the Kevill-Davies, sold the castle to the Trustees of Sir James Croft, 11th Baronet, then a minor. The Crofts are still in residence at the castle, although the buildings and grounds are cared for by the National Trust and are open to the public.

Croft Castle

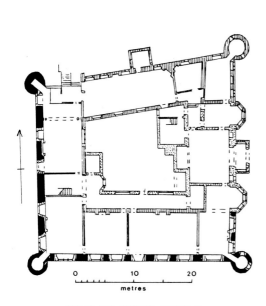

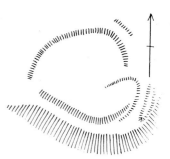

PLAN OF CUSOP CASTLE

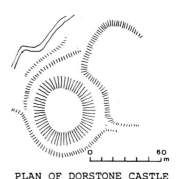

PLAN OF DORSTONE CASTLE

PLAN OF CROFT CASTLE

The medieval castle measured 30m from east to west within walls up to about 1.2m thick. The south corners are right angles but the east wall extends rather further north than does the west wall. At each corner is a round turret about 3.3m in diameter containing tiny round rooms. It is likely that the original medieval hall was in the west range, but no medieval openings or other features now survive in any of the four ranges around the central courtyard. The northern range was rebuilt in the 16th century and now contains a kitchen and a library. The east range is of c1750-60, and the porch and the existing parapet and gables on the south front are of 1913. There are numerous Elizabethan and Georgian windows. The west wing was continued northwards by a 17th century extension demolished in 1937. The moats were probably filled in during the 18th century.

CUBLINGTON CASTLE
SO 406384

The badly damaged mound at Castle Farm is probably the site of the castle of Cublington held by the De La Field family.

CUSOP CASTLE
SO 239414

SW of the church is a large enclosure with a surrounding ditch and steep natural slopes to the SW and south. Cusop belonged to the Clavenogh family but was held by Henry ap Griffith in the early 14th century.

DORSTONE CASTLE SO 312417

West of the village are the earthworks of one of the chief castles
protecting the Golden Valley. No stone buildings remain, and there
is no certain evidence there ever were any, but the site remained
in use by the Solaris family throughout the 13th and 14th centuries.
They were knights serving the Mortimers of Wigmore. In 1403 Henry
IV ordered Sir Walter Fitz-Walter to fortify the castle against the
Welsh. Dorstone passed to the de la Mares in the 15th century, and
then to the Lysters, who sold it to the Aubreys in Elizabeth I's
reign, whilst in 1780 it was sold to the Cornwalls. The motte rises
10m to a summit measuring 35m by 30m and to the NE are signs of a
bailey platform protected on the north and NW by a small stream.

DOWNTON-ON-THE-ROCK CASTLE SO 427735

The small mound has a depression on the summit with stone debris,
probably the remains of a stone building of uncertain date.

EARDISLAND CASTLE & MOTTE SO 421586 and 419588

North of the church is a tree-clad mound with a summit diameter of
about 27m rising 5m above a wet moat crossed by a causeway on the
NW side. This was a seat of the Pembridges and Twyfords. At Monk's
Court on the other side of the river is a second mound 1.5m high.

EARDISLEY CASTLE SO 311491

The rectangular moated enclosure measuring about 95m by 75m with a
motte in the SW corner is assumed to be the site of Roger de Lacy's
'domus defensabilis' mentioned in Domesday Book. There are signs
of an outer enclosure to the west. The de Bohun Earls of Hereford
were later overlords of Eardisley until their main line died out
in 1372, but the castle was occupied by tenants. In 1263 Roger de
Clifford was in possession, and it was here that he imprisoned the
unpopular foreign Bishop of Hereford, Peter de Aquablanca.

In 1272 William Baskerville was licensed to have services in
the chapel of Eardisley Castle, and the place formed the principal
residence of the Baskervilles until their fortunes declined in the
early 17th century. Henry IV ordered Nicholas Montgomery to fortify
the castle against the Welsh in 1403. Most of the buildings were
demolished during the Civil War, although the last Baskerville
occupied the gatehouse in a state of poverty until 1670, when the
estate passed to William Barnesley. The existing farmhouse in the
middle of the enclosure dates only from the 18th century.

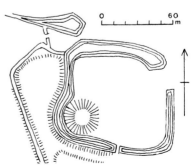

PLAN OF EARDISLEY CASTLE

EATON TREGOZ CASTLE

This castle in the parish of Foy has now totally disappeared. It was the seat of the Tregoz family in the 12th and 13th centuries, and the castle chapel is mentioned in 1280. When John Tregoz died in c1300 the castle passed to William de Grandison who in 1309 was licensed to crenellate it. In 1375 it went to the Watertons, and in the early 15th century it passed to the Abrahalls, who remained in possession until 1673.

ECCLESWALL CASTLE   SO 653234

Nothing now remains of the castle, which was the Talbots' original seat until they obtained Goodrich Castle in 1326.

ELLINGHAM CASTLE

This is yet another castle which has vanished. The name Quarry Wood given to the site by Blount in the 17th century suggests that it was then being plundered for building materials. The name derives from the Helyon family, who held it from the Audleys.

EWYAS HAROLD CASTLE   SO 384287

Osbern Pentecost built a castle here in c1050. It was re-fortified by William Fitz-Osbern in 1067-71, and at the time of Domesday was held by the original builder's nephew Alfred of Marlborough. Ewyas Harold passed by marriage to Robert Tregoz in the 13th century, and after John Tregoz died in c1300 it passed by marriage to Roger de la Warre. It was his grandson Sir Roger de la Warre that took King John of France prisoner at Poitiers in 1356. Henry IV in 1403 gave the castle to Sir Phillip le Vache with the intention that it should be re-fortified against the Welsh, but later the same year custody of it was given to Sir William Beauchamp, Lord Bergavenny, from whose heirs it passed to the Nevilles. The castle played no further part in history and in 1645 was noted as "ruynous and gone".

The castle comprises a large bailey strongly sited on the end of a spur with a huge, mostly natural, mound facing the higher ground to the north, from which it is divided by a deep ditch. The mound never had a ditch towards the bailey, and its slopes are now covered with trees. The mound summit 32m across is less heavily covered with vegetation. The debris and quarry pits on the summit indicate the former presence of a shell wall which is said to have been 3m thick. It is probable that there were round flanking towers as at Clifford Castle. There is no evidence that any of the owners went to the expense of walling the bailey in stone, but the chapel dedicated to St Nicholas which lay within it may have been a stone building.

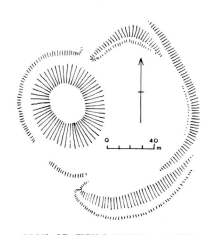

PLAN OF EWYAS HAROLD CASTLE

GOODRICH CASTLE SO 577200

The castle almost certainly takes its name from Godric Mapplestone, who held Hulle (Howl) nearby at the time of Domesday. He is assumed to have built it in the 1090s and it is mentioned as Godric's Castle in 1101-2. William Fitz-Baderon, Lord of Monmouth, held Goodrich in 1144, possibly having illegally seized it during the anarchy of Stephen's reign. It may have been he who built the small tower keep. Goodrich was later a Crown possession and the Pipe Rolls note expenditure on the castle in 1178, but in 1201 King John granted it to William Marshall, Earl of Pembroke. After the death of his son Walter at Goodrich in 1245 the castle reverted to the Crown and in 1247 was granted to William de Valence, who was married to Joan de Munchesney, co-heiress to the Marshall estates, and who was created Earl of Pembroke. It was he and his son Aymer who rebuilt Goodrich Castle into its present form, and they used it as a convenient half way stopping place between their English and Welsh estates.

Aymer Valance's rights at Goodrich passed on his death in 1324 to his niece Elizabeth Comyn. She was abducted by Hugh Despencer the younger and forced to resign her rights to him. She later married Richard Talbot, and after the fall of Edward II and the Despencers late in 1326 he seized the castle, which was subsequently confirmed to him and his wife. The castle formed the principal residence of his successors, who became Earls of Shrewsbury in 1446. The third Earl, John, being a Lancastrian, was forfeited in 1461 and Goodrich was held by William Herbert until the Earl was reconciled to Edward IV and re-instated to his estates. The Earls of Shrewsbury later developed other residences elsewhere and Goodrich was little used during the latter part of the 16th century. It was unoccupied in 1616, when the 7th Earl, Gilbert Talbot, died and the castle passed to his daughter Elizabeth and her husband, Henry Grey, Earl of Kent.

In 1643 the castle was garrisoned for Parliament by the Earl of Stamford, but on his withdrawal from the area the Royalists were able to take possession. As Parliament's strength grew during 1645 the garrison under Sir Henry Lingen found itself very isolated, although they were able to cause considerable disruption to local communications. A surprise attack succeeded in burning the stables in the outer bailey and at the beginning of June 1646 Colonel John Birch began a regular siege. The mortar Roaring Meg, now at Hereford, caused much damage to the castle, especially to the cisterns, and the water supply from outside was cut off. Mining and countermining were employed but after part of the NW tower collapsed and blocked a counter mine, leaving a breach, Lingen and his garrison of about 170 men surrendered on 31st July, and the castle was then slighted.

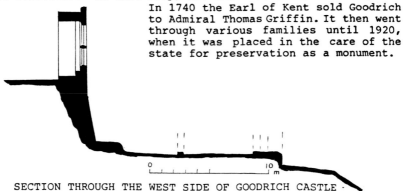

In 1740 the Earl of Kent sold Goodrich to Admiral Thomas Griffin. It then went through various families until 1920, when it was placed in the care of the state for preservation as a monument.

SECTION THROUGH THE WEST SIDE OF GOODRICH CASTLE ·

The form of the original castle is uncertain, the rocky site being ill suited to defences of earth and timber. The earliest part of the present building is the tower keep of c1150, the smallest surviving example of its type, being just 4.5m square within ashlar faced walls 2.2m thick with shallow buttresses at the corners and middle of each side. It is 16.5m high and contained a cellar, hall, or living room, and a bedroom. The existing roof is flat but it is assumed that the original was gabled, with the apex roughly at the height of the now destroyed wall-walk. The original doorway, now converted into a window, is at hall level, and until a doorway was broken through at ground level the basement was reached only by a trapdoor and ladder from above, and lighted by a single loop. From the hall a spiral stair in the NW corner rises to the upper levels. A string course with chevron ornament marks the top storey, which has two-light round-arched windows to the west and north.

The Marshalls evidently added a stone walled court to the keep in the early 13th century. All that has survived the rebuilding is some of the east curtain wall, part of the footings of a round SW tower within the much larger tower now there, and the reset piscina of the chapel. The remainder was probably begun in the 1280s, when oaks were sent from the Forest of Dean, and continued into the 14th century. Walls about 2.5m thick were built around a rectangular court with ranges of buildings on each side, a gatehouse at the NE corner, and round towers with tall spurs at the other three corners.

The gateway is approached by a ramp which formerly had a turning bridge at the inner end. The passageway was closed by at least two sets of doors, and two portcullises, and there is a machicolation from the room above. On the north side of the passage is a mural corridor to a latrine and a small porter's room formed in the base of a round turret, whilst on the south side is the chapel which has a polygonal apse set within a rounded outer section. The large mullioned window in the apse is a later insertion. Adjoining the chapel is a polygonal stair turret serving the fine upper chambers.

Goodrich Castle: The NW tower from the keep.

Goodrich Castle: The SW tower.

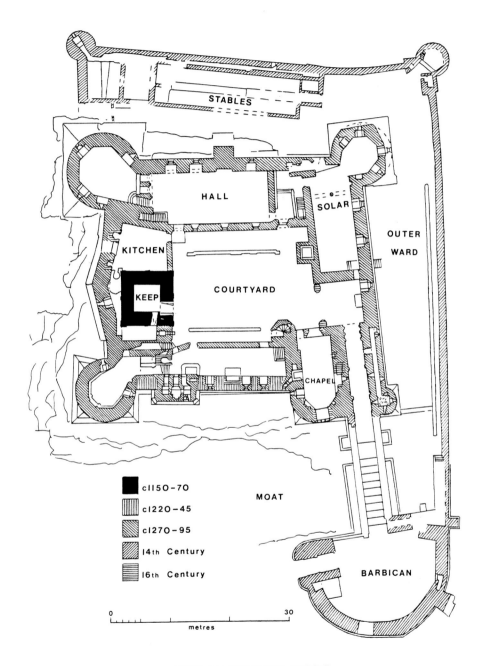

STABLES

HALL

SOLAR

OUTER WARD

KITCHEN

KEEP

COURTYARD

CHAPEL

■ c1150-70

▨ c1220-45

▧ c1270-95

▨ 14th Century

▤ 16th Century

MOAT

BARBICAN

0   30

metres

PLAN OF GOODRICH CASTLE

Goodrich Castle: The Gateway.

The gateway passage opens into a square space later enclosed
to form rooms above. This leads into the north end of a rectangular
courtyard, along the east and west sides of which were formerly
low lean-to roofed corridors. The east range was probably used by
retainers and had another storey added to it later. A projection
from the east wall contains a complex series of latrines. The hall
occupies the west range with an ante-room separating it from the
solar in the north range. The solar west end was divided off by a
pair of arches carried on a pier continued down through a chamber
below, beneath the courtyard level. Bedrooms were provided in the
NW tower, which is now very ruined, and a small private chapel lay
over the ante-room. In the thick outer walls the hall and solar
have long transomed single light windows set in wide embrasures
with seats. The keep occupies the middle part of the south range,
with the curtain projected out as a spur behind it. To the east is
a vaulted prison, and to the west is a kitchen with several ovens.
Beyond these are long flights of steps to the uppermost rooms in
the southern towers, which were large and pleasant rooms provided
with fireplaces, and intended for important officials or guests.
The castle is built on a knob of sandstone using material taken
from the very deep and impressive ditch around the south and east
sides. On the other sides is a shelf of level land forming an outer
court, and containing extensive stables on the west. Beyond the
thin enclosing wall, which has round turrets on the west corners
and is reduced to its foundations, the ground falls steeply to the
River Wye on the north, and to a brook on the west. On the eastern
side, beyond the ramp to the gatehouse, is a semi-circular barbican
with thick walls and its own narrow rock-cut ditch. This barbican
is strikingly similar to another built at the Tower of London in
1279, although like the outer court it may be as late as c1310-20.

Hampton Court.

HAMPTON COURT
SO 515527

The de Hamptons had a manor house here in the 13th century but the present mansion was built by Rowland Lenthall from the proceeds of the ransoms of prisoners he took at Agincourt in 1415. The original crenellations, long since rebuilt, were licensed in 1434. Leland says that Rowland ceased building operations after the death of his only son, but there is nothing in the structure to confirm this. Rowland's daughter married Thomas Cornwall, whose grandson sold the mansion in c1510 to Sir Humphrey Coningsby. His descendant Thomas was created Lord Coningsby by William III in 1692 as a reward for good service, and in the early 18th century he commissioned Colin Campbell to rebuild the house. Further remodelling was undertaken after the house was sold to Richard Arkright in 1808.

The house has four irregular ranges set around a rectangular central court. Much of the building now dates from the 18th and 19th centuries and the chief medieval survivals are the substantial gatehouse on the north, the lower parts of the north ranges with small rectangular turrets at the ends, the chapel which projects eastwards from the north end of the east front, and the porch in the middle of the north side of the south range, which originally led into the screens passage at the west end of the hall. All the windows in these portions are later replacements. The upper part of the north front has rainwater heads dated 1710 with the arms of the first Lord Coningsby and his second wife Frances Jones.

Widemarsh Gate, Hereford

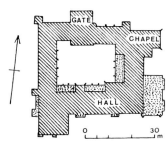

PLAN OF HAMPTON COURT

HEREFORD CASTLE

Ralph, Earl of Hereford, built a castle at Hereford in c1050 which lasted only until 1055, when it was destroyed by the Welsh. It was perhaps smaller than the large motte and bailey castle which in 1067 William Fitz-Osbern raised on or near the same site. Geoffrey Talbot held Hereford against King Stephen, who besieged and took the town and castle in 1138 after a siege of about a month. Talbot returned in 1140 with Miles of Gloucester, and retook the castle after a vigorous siege in which it was bombarded with stones from a siege engine mounted on the cathedral tower and an unsuccessful attempt was made by Stephen to relieve it. Miles, who was created Earl of Hereford by the Empress Matilda in 1141, later caused much offence to the Church when he had a ditch and rampart cut through part of the cemetery of the collegiate church of St Guthlac, which lay in the castle bailey, and many bodies were left exposed.

On his accession in 1154 Henry II confirmed Miles' son Roger in possession of Hereford Castle, only to take it back when the latter rebelled the following year. The castle was then maintained as a royal stronghold. In 1165 and 1169 the houses on the motte, presumably still of wood, were repaired, but at some unknown period between then and the 1240s they were replaced by a large stone tower keep. The castle was strengthened at the time of the 1173-4 rebellion by Henry's sons, and the bailey defences were at least partly of stone by 1181-2, when a defective section of walling was demolished and rebuilt. Further work was carried out during Prince John's revolt in 1191-3. John as King had a small tower built in 1202-3, timber for hoards was sent to the garrison in 1213, and the castle was fortified against the Welsh in 1215-6.

It was probably Henry III who surrounded the tower keep with a court with several towers. Leland says that there were ten towers, but Speed's map of 1610 suggests a more likely number of about six. Leland's total may include those on the circuit of the bailey wall. There is no specific mention of such a substantial new work in the royal accounts, but continual repairs are noted, and a new tower was built in 1239-40 to replace a fallen one. Despite over £100 being spent on Hereford Castle in 1250-2 a survey of 1254 reported that the keep roof needed repair, and the steps up to it needed to be entirely rebuilt, the Jews' prison below the wall around the keep was roofless, the two gatehouses needed repair, and much of the wall facing the Wye was being undermined by the river. A quay was subsequently built to solve the latter problem.

Much is recorded of the domestic buildings at this time, all of which have now vanished. The bailey contained the King's great hall, the King's small hall, the county hall, private chambers for the King and Queen and their knights, an almonry, a counting house or treasury, a stable, two gaols, a building which housed siege engines, and various offices including a kitchen and bakery. In 1245 the King's chamber was whitewashed and wainscoted, whilst the Queen's chamber was lengthened, wainscoted, painted, and provided with a wardrobe, fireplace and latrine. A chapel built beside the King's chamber in 1233 was already in need of repair by 1254. It was probably this chapel that was rebuilt in 1283-4. A new kitchen for the King's household was built in 1256, and in the 1260s a new chamber was built for the royal clerks.

Hereford supported Simon de Montfort and withstood an attack by Roger Mortimer in 1264. In 1265 de Montfort governed England from the city whilst Henry III and Prince Edward were kept in the castle. Edward was allowed to ride outside the walls and he escaped to Wigmore after organising races to tire out his guards' mounts.

Hereford Castle was little used after the defeat of the Welsh and surveys of 1291 and 1300 record several roofs as needing repair and that a section of the outer wall had collapsed. It seems that some repairs were made but it was not until 1402, during Glyndwr's revolt, that further major repairs were undertaken. A long section of the river wall had collapsed and the breach was filled with a paling made from 351 oaks felled in Haywood Forest, whilst the keep was re-roofed and other towers and turrets patched up. Leland in c1540 described Hereford Castle as having been "one of the fairest, largest, and strongest castles in England", but comments that it now "tendeth toward ruin". He describes the "great bridge of stone arches, and a drawbridge in the middle of it", which formed the approach to a twin towered gatehouse on the north side as "now clean down", and also mentions the spring which provided the water supply and the mill inside the bailey driven by a brook coming out of the wet moat.

The castle does not seem to have played an independent part during the sieges and occupations of the city in the Civil War and merely formed part of the defensive circuit. It appears, however, to have suffered considerable damage at this time and most of what remained was demolished in 1660. A map made in 1677 shows only the motte, the moats, the main gatehouse, and the watergate. The motte was later entirely removed, and also the main gatehouse, but the building remaining in the west corner of the bailey appears to incorporate parts of the 13th century watergate, although it has no features in it of much interest. The large bailey became a public park in the 18th century and the ramparts on the north and eastern sides appear to be at least partly of that era. The east moat is dry but the northern arm of the moat still retains water. In 1960 excavations revealed the foundations of a small Norman church, presumably that of St Guthlac, which still stood in Speed's time.

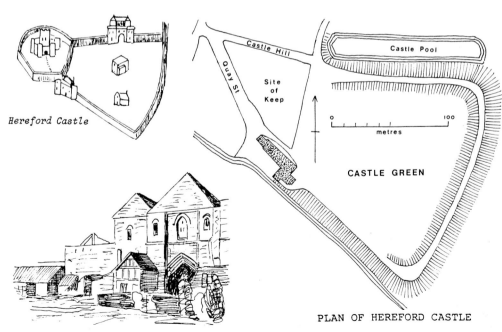

Hereford Castle

Bye Street Gate, Hereford

PLAN OF HEREFORD CASTLE

HEREFORD CITY WALLS

Excavations have revealed remains of a timber revetted rampart and ditch dating from the 9th century. It appears to have enclosed an almost square area north of the Wye with the cathedral occupying the SW quarter, and a cross pattern of streets with main gates in the middle of the sides. The defended area was later extended to the east to enclose the church of St Guthlac, and in the early 10th century the rampart was externally faced in stone, although probably still with a wooden superstructure. The defences appear to have been in a neglected state at the time of the Welsh attack of 1055 when the city was sacked and the cathedral burnt.

The charter granted to the city in 1189 and the threat of more trouble from the Welsh prompted considerable new work on defences in the 1190s. Four new gatehouses, probably of timber, were built, and the enclosed area was extended to the north, whilst the Row Ditch south of the river may be a work of this period to protect a suburb there. The town was held in the interest of Prince John in 1197 and had to be besieged and captured by the Justiciar Hubert Walter. Henry III, who was at Hereford in 1223, evidently regarded the defences as inadequate, and he authorised the bailiffs to exact tolls on merchandise coming into the city for the purpose of building the stone walls which were probably begun in 1224-5. The wall was built in front of the older rampart and had in front a deep wet moat fed by the Yazor Brook. The wall was up to 2m thick and 5.5m high, flanked by 17 semi-circular bastions rising above it, and had six stone gatehouses. One stood at the south end of the bridge over the Wye, and the others closed off St Nicholas Street (Friars' Gate), Eign Street, Widemarsh Street, Bye Street, and St Owen's Street.

In spite of the cost of maintenance the walls appear to have been kept in a reasonable condition throughout the later medieval period, and Leland found them in good order. By his time individual citizens were each expected to maintain a short section, called a loop. In 1596 a bastion near St Owen's Gate was rented to William Wellington on condition that he kept it in repair. However it would appear that the walls required considerable repairs to make them defensible in the Civil War. The city was surrendered to roving Parliamentary armies in October 1642 and April 1643 without much resistance, but a royalist garrison under Barnaby Scudamore made a much more determined defence against a Scottish army under the Earl of Leven in the summer of 1645. The city finally fell into the hands of Parliament when Colonel Birch made a surprise attack on Bye Street Gate in December 1645. The circuit of the walls remained almost intact when Taylor's map was made in 1757, but the gateways were destroyed at the end of the 18th century, and subsequently much of the walls themselves were robbed for their materials.

The roads carrying the traffic around the NE, north, and west sides of the centre of the city follow the line of the defences and occupy the site of the former moat. Considerable sections of the north and NE sections of the wall are marked out by thin walling of comparatively recent date. Most of it is low, but parts are quite lofty. Genuine original portions of the wall now only remain on the west side of the city. A considerable section about 2m high with one round bastion remains between the sites of Eign Gate and Friars' Gate, and the next section reaching almost to the river is better preserved. It has small pilaster buttresses possibly indicating a date earlier than Henry III's reign, and is nowhere more than 1m thick at present. It has a second round bastion still 6m high with arrow loops in the upper parts of the walls.

Hereford City Wall.

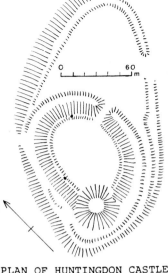

0   60
m

PLAN OF HUNTINGDON CASTLE

HUNTINGTON CASTLE   SO 249539

The remote parish of Huntington is enclosed by Wales on all sides
except to the NE. There are two castle sites, Turret Castle 1km
east of the church, and Huntington Castle 0.5km north of the church.
It is likely that the stronghold established by Bernard de Newmarch
in this area in the late 11th century was at Turret Castle, and
the other site was constructed by the de Braose family to whom the
lordship passed in the 12th century. In 1248 Huntington passed to
the de Bohun Earls of Hereford, and in 1264 the castle was captured
by Prince Edward from Humphrey de Bohun.
     The male line of the de Bohuns failed in 1372, and the heiress
married Henry, Earl of Derby, son of John of Gaunt. When he took
the throne in 1399 as Henry IV the earldom of Hereford passed over
to Edward Stafford, Earl of Buckingham. He was killed fighting for
Henry IV at the battle of Shrewsbury in 1403. Later the same year
his widow Anne refortified the castle against the Welsh, the keep
being re-roofed, the main gate and postern gate re-hung on fresh
hinges, and a new outer ditch and palisade constructed. However,
the Staffords had little use for the castle after then. It was said
to be worth nothing in 1460, but one tower was still used as a gaol
in 1521 when the Stafford estates were surveyed on the execution
and forfeiture of the Duke of Buckingham by Henry VIII. In this
survey the castle is referred to as the stone castle, as opposed to
the original timber castle on the other site. In 1564 Elizabeth I
gave the manor to Sir Ambrose Cave. He later sold it to Sir Francis
Vaughan, and the estate subsequently passed through the Garner,
Townsend, Holman, and Cheese families.
     The castle lies overlooking a tributary of the Gladestry Brook.
It has an oval bailey measuring about 75m by 60m with a rampart and
ditch. A motte lies at the south end, and an outer bailey to the
NE. In the 13th century a keep, probably a round tower, was built
on the mound, and stone walls were built around the bailey. These
still mostly survived as late as 1670, but there now only remain
buried footings on the 9m high motte, a high fragment of the west
curtain wall near the mound, and a fragment of a mural tower on the
north. The site is now very overgrown and difficult to inspect.

29

KENTCHURCH COURT

SO 421270

The 3m high mound in Bowlstone Court Wood on the hillside 1.3km to the north of the church, and the moated site to the east of the church probably mark the sites of older manorial seats than the 14th century castle which lies hidden away in a side valley nearby. Kentchurch was long held by the Scudamores, who gradually altered the castle into a comfortable country mansion. Substantial parts of the old castle remain, especially the NW tower, the NE range, and the SE gateway. Although heightened in c1800 by Nash and then provided with large mullioned windows in each of the four storeys above the basement, the NW tower is an important relic. It has a latrine projecting from the NE corner at third storey level. The medieval hall lay in the east range. A medieval range south of it was remodelled in c1700, and again in c1800 by Nash.

KILPECK CASTLE

SO 444305

William Fitz-Norman built Kilpeck Castle in the late 11th century as the administrative centre of the district of Archenfield. His grandson Henry took the surname de Kilpeck, and Henry's son John purchased the barony of Pulverbatch in Shropshire in 1193. Kilpeck Castle is mentioned in the royal Pipe Rolls for 1189, while King John was entertained within it in 1211 and 1212. It is presumed that by that period the buildings on the mound had been rebuilt in stone. On the death of Hugh de Kilpeck in the mid 13th century Kilpeck passed to his younger daughter Isabella who married William de Waleraund. William was succeeded by Alan Plunkenet, whose son Alan died childless in 1325, after which Kilpeck passed by marriage to the Bohuns. Edward IV granted Kilpeck to his sister and her husband James Butler, 1st Earl of Ormond, although it was regranted later to Sir William Herbert, 1st Earl of Pembroke. It is unlikely either lord ever used the castle which by then was probably in an advanced state of decay. Leland's comment on the building is that "some ruins of the walls yet stand", but it is said to have been briefly occupied during the Civil War and to have been slighted in 1645 by Parliamentary forces. The owners in the 17th century were the Pye family of Saddlebow and The Mynde.

The castle earthworks lie between the small but splendid church of c1140 to the east and a hollow to the west. They consist of a motte rising about 6m to a summit 28m in diameter with a large semi-circular bailey to the east. There is an outer bank to the motte ditch on the NW side, where there is an oval outer enclosure, and there are indications of another enclosure to the south, and of a rectangular village enclosure to the east. On the motte summit are two fragments of a shell keep wall about 2m thick and 5m high. Both have the remains of round backed fireplace flues of former internal lean-to buildings. There are no signs of any stone buildings or defences in the bailey and the shell on the motte was probably big enough to form a self contained fortified residence.

KINGSLAND CASTLE

SO 445613

West of the church is a mound about 5m high with a summit diameter of about 40m. According to Leland part of a long abandoned stone keep (probably a shell wall) was still standing on the summit in the early 16th century. Rather feeble ditches mark out the extent of two large baileys to the NE and east. It is assumed that the castle, which was a Mortimer possession, was originally protected by extensive marshland and wide water-filled moats.

30

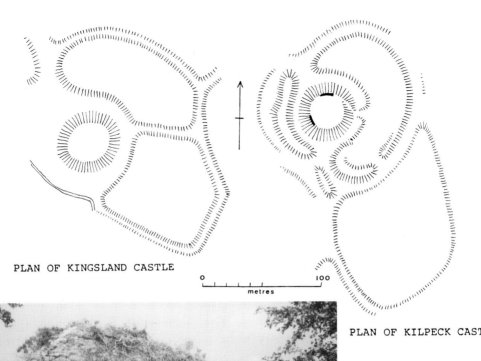

PLAN OF KINGSLAND CASTLE

PLAN OF KILPECK CASTLE

o | | | | | 100
metres

Kilpeck Castle:
The Shell Keep.

KINGTON CASTLE SO 291569

On the edge of a steep slope above the Back Brook to the north
of the church are slight traces of the ramparts and ditches of a
castle which is mentioned in the Pipe Roll for 1187, and descended
in later years with the lordship of Huntingdon.

KINNERSLEY CASTLE SO 346497

The Kinnersley family had a castle or moated manor house here which
passed to Richard de la Bere in c1340, and to the Lyster family in
the late 16th century. The present tall L-plan house with three
storeys above cellars, set immediately east of the church, was built
by Roger Vaughan in c1585-90. It passed to Francis Smallman in 1633.
Medieval masonry may survive in the staircase tower and there are
slight traces of the former surrounding moat.

31

LINGEN CASTLE AND RINGWORK   SO 366673 and 372681

Immediately north of the church is a rectangular bailey platform
measuring 90m by 60m, with a pond in the middle, and to the east a
moated mound 6.5m high with a summit 18m across. A kilometer to
the NE is a ringwork about 35m in diameter with traces of a bailey
platform extending to the SE.

LLANCILLO CASTLE   SO 367256

East of the church is a mound bearing the last traces of a stone
shell keep about 16m in external diameter. There is no bailey.

LONGTOWN CASTLE   SO 321292

Longtown Castle was probably constructed by Gilbert de Lacy in the
1140s or 50s. It is likely to be the 'new castle' mentioned in the
Pipe Rolls of 1187-8, which would make the motte and bailey down at
Ponthendre the old castle of Ewyas Lacy then also mentioned. There
are reasons for assuming that the stone keep and bailey wall were
built by Walter de Lacy during the period 1216-31, when he was the
sheriff of Herefordshire. Henry III was at Longtown in 1233, and
in the following year the castle was aquired by John Fitz-Geoffrey
when he married the widow of Walter de Lacy's only son Gilbert.
The castle later passed to Walter's daughter Margaret who married
John de Verdon. When their grandson Theobald died in 1316 Longtown
passed by marriage to Bartholomew de Berghersh. His son Bartholomew
died in 1369, and the castle passed by marriage to the Despencers,
and then to the Beauchamps and Nevilles. These families all lived
elsewhere and Longtown Castle was probably left to decay from the
end of the 13th century, except for a brief period around 1403 when
Henry IV ordered it refortified against the Welsh.
     The castle consists of a round tower keep on top of a mound, a
pentagonal inner bailey with a square bailey beyond it to the south,
and a rectangular outer court to the east with high ramparts. The
overall square shape suggests a Roman origin for the outer defences
but no proof of this has yet been discovered. Dividing the baileys
is a wall 1.8m thick now about 4m high. It appears to have been
built against a bank, and presumably had a ditch in front of it. A
gateway passage 1.8m wide with grooves for a portcullis lies near
the east end. The 3m thick walls flanking the passage have rounded
outer ends and thus formed solid turrets. Only fragments remain
of the eastern wall of the inner bailey and nothing at all of the
western wall, where there is now a hedge overlooking a steep slope.
Of the outer bailey wall there are foundations on the south and a
few fragments on the east beside remains of a much later building.

Longtown Castle:
The Bailey Gateway.

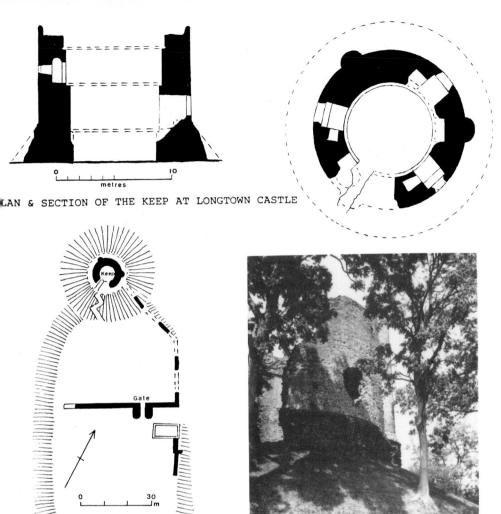

PLAN & SECTION OF THE KEEP AT LONGTOWN CASTLE

PLAN OF LONGTOWN CASTLE

The Keep, Longtown Castle.

The keep measures 13.3m in diameter above a high and deeply battered plinth, most of which is now broken away. Spaced evenly around the exterior were three semi-circular buttresses. One, now destroyed, contained a spiral stair and had the entrance next to it, another contains a latrine opening off the top room, and the third backs onto where there is a fireplace in the hall. This keep was once thought to contain just a hall and a dark bedroom above but recent clearence has shown that there was also a low unlit basement. The hall has three windows which were once of two narrow lights with square heads under a round outer arch. That facing NE has rosettes on the outer face. The embrasures each have a locker in one jamb. The two top storey windows are mere narrow loops.

LYDE CASTLE

On a low lying site which was probably once protected by wet moats and marshland are slight earthworks remaining of a castle belonging to one of the knights of the Bishops of Hereford. The castle is mentioned in a document of Henry III's reign.

LYONSHALL CASTLE

It is likely that this castle was founded soon after the Conquest by the de Lacys. It is probably one of the two castles belonging to John D'Evreux which are mentioned in the Pipe Roll for 1188, and it is mentioned as "Lenhaul" in 1209. The Devereux or D'Ebroicis family originally held the castle from the de Lacys and Stephen D'Ebroicis is thought to have built the round keep at Lyonshall in c1220-7 in imitation of his Overlord Walter de Lacy's new keep at Longtown. During the reign of Edward I Lyonshall formed the chief seat of William Touchet, and it was a possession of Bartholomew de Badlesmere at the time of his execution by Edward II in 1322. It later passed by marriage to John de Vere, Earl of Oxford, and from 1386 until his execution in 1388 was held by Sir Simon Burley. It then reverted to Sir John Devereux, who died in 1393, leaving an heiress who married Walter, 5th Baron Fitz-Walter. He was ordered by Henry IV to garrison the castle against the Welsh in 1403. From the mid 15th century until 1641 Lyonshall was back in the hands of the Devereux family. It then passed to the Thynnes, who sold it to the Cheese family, but it was by then a long-neglected ruin.

The circular inner bailey, now very overgrown, lies in trees close to the church. It measures about 45m in diameter within a thick wall of which only fragments and buried foundations remain. It is surrounded by a wet moat crossed by a timber bridge to the SE, and lies within the SW end of a rectangular outer bailey, while there is a third, almost square, enclosure beyond to the NE. The moats of these outer enclosures are incomplete and now only partly water filled. There is no evidence that they ever had buildings or walls of stone. On the north side of the inner bailey the wall projects out as a more thinly walled polygonal mantlet or chemise around the base of a round tower keep 12.6m in external diameter with walls 2.8m thick above a sloping plinth with a roll moulding at the top. There are three gaps representing basement window loops, and a wider gap on the south where the entrance and staircase were.

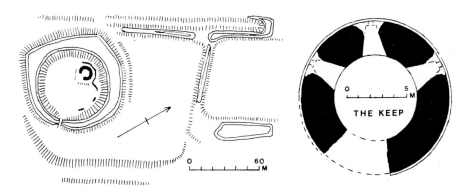

PLANS OF LYONSHALL CASTLE

MOCCAS CASTLE
SO 348426

The last traces of the castle earthworks have now disappeared. It is thought to have had a round keep, but the licence to crenellate granted to Sir Hugh de Freyne in 1293 specified that the outer wall was not to be more than 3m high below the battlements and was to be without towers or turrets. The property had recently been taken into Crown possession for a short while, possibly because Sir Hugh had illegally begun work on fortifications without a licence. The Frenes lived here at least until the death of Richard Frene in the 1370s, but in the mid 15th century Edward ap Meredith held Moccas, and from the mid 16th century the Vaughans were in possession.

MOUSE CASTLE
SO 247424

This hilltop earthwork lies in woodland 1km NE of Cusop. The oval enclosure has steep slopes on all sides except to the NE, where there is a double rampart. In the middle is the motte, the earthen slopes of which have been quarried away leaving a rocky core with faces about 2m high.

MUCH MARCLE CASTLE
SO 657328

The 15th century west tower of the church is reputed to have been constructed from materials taken from a stone castle built on the earthworks immediately to the north. The castle is mentioned in the 12th century, and was held by the Mortimers in the 13th and 14th centuries. Elizabeth I sold the site to the Kyrle family, who held it throughout the 17th century. The mound rises 6.5m to a summit about 30m in diameter. There are several buildings of late date within the moated bailey platform to the east, and an outer court lay to the east and north.

NEWTON MOTTE
SO 293441

This low lying site guards the northern entrance to the Golden Valley. A moated mound 4.5m high stands in one corner of a roughly rectangular bailey now weakly defended, but probably once provided with wet moats fed from the Bach Brook.

OLD CASTLETON MOTTE
SO 283457

This site is thought to have been the original stronghold of the lordship of Clifford founded by William Fitz-Osbern, and abandoned in favour of the stone castle site during the first half of the 12th century. It consists of a kidney shaped bailey defended by a rampart and ditch, and a worn down motte on the north side. There are large outer platforms to the east and west which are mostly of natural origin, and there was once marshland below to the north.

ORCOP CASTLE
SO 473265

The motte and its kidney shaped bailey to the north are low lying, but probably once had wide wet moats filled by the adjacent stream. The mound rises 6.5m to a summit 20m in diameter, and the bailey measures about 75m from east to west by 60m from north to south.

PEMBRIDGE CASTLE

The castle takes its name from the Pembridge family whose original
seat was at the village of that name in northern Herefordshire.
The earliest parts may have been built by Ralph de Pembridge, who
died in 1219. The castle later passed to the Mortimers and in 1387
Sir Richard Burley died in possession of it. In 1445 the castle
passed to the Hoptons, and was later held by the Baynhams, who sold
it to Sir Walter Pye. Unlike many other Herefordshire castles that
at Pembridge was maintained, improved, and inhabited until autumn
1644 when Edward Massey, the Parliamentary governor of Gloucester,
occupied parts of Monmouthshire, and installed a garrison in it.

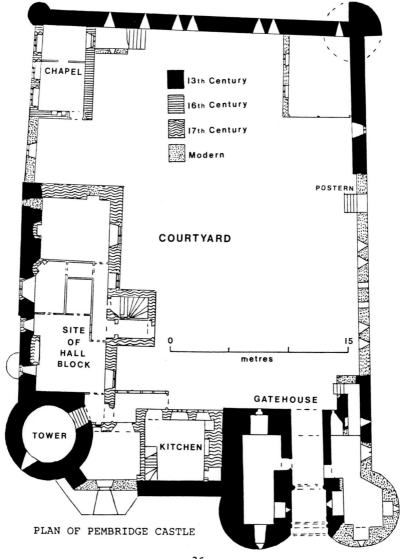

PLAN OF PEMBRIDGE CASTLE

Pembridge Castle: The Gatehouse   *Pembridge Castle*

The buildings were severely damaged during or after a fortnight's siege and capture of the castle by Colonel Scudamore, but were subsequently purchased, repaired, and inhabited by George Kemble. In 1715 it was occupied by Henry Scudamore and later passed to the Townleys of Lancashire, who sold it to the Baileys. The castle had by then become neglected, and it was heavily restored for further use as a residence in the early 20th century.

The castle lies on a sloping site and is surrounded by a moat, to retain the water of which a substantial outer bank has been created on the NW and NE sides. The building comprises a curtain wall with an average thickness of 1.4m enclosing a rectangular court about 27m wide by 36m long. At the west corner is a four storey round tower thought to date from c1195-1210, and regarded as a keep, although it measures only 7.5m in external diameter and is without internal staircases. There are several small original loops, and a projecting garderobe on the south side. The square headed fire-place on the top storey may also be original. Adjoining this tower was a contemporary block, later replaced by an early 17th century house which is still habitable. The house has a projection towards the court containing the entrance and staircase. Of the same era are the kitchen and larder between the west tower and the gatehouse.

The gatehouse and curtain walls are probably of c1260-1300. The gateway passage was closed by a portcullis and doors, and flanked by round towers about 6.5m in diameter. The western tower has a rectangular portion the same width towards the court, but the much rebuilt eastern tower has a thinner portion behind so that the SE curtain wall is flanked by the round part. On the upper storey of the gatehouse is a fireplace of c1400. The central part of the SE curtain was destroyed in 1644 and the thinner and lower walling in this part now leaves the house exposed to view from the hillside, which was not originally the case. At the east corner is a round turret with hollow segments lower down towards the court and either side of the curtain walls. The north corner has a tiny round turret and there is the base of another close to the west tower on the NW side. Within the north corner is a 16th century chapel with three 17th century windows pierced through the NW curtain wall, and an older tunnel-vaulted undercroft below.

Penyard Castle

PONTHENDRE MOTTE   SO 326281

The high moated mound with a bailey platform extending between it
and the Olchon Beck to the NE is probably the original 11th century
castle of the lordship of Ewyas Lacy, later known as Longtown.

PENYARD CASTLE   SO 618226

This castle is first mentioned in 1338, when repairs were made. It
was then a Talbot possession and the family may have had a house
here as early as Henry II's reign. In the early 15th century it was
a residence of Sir Lewis Talbot, son of the Earl of Shrewsbury, and
there was a mint at the castle in the 16th century. On the death
of Gilbert Talbot, 7th Earl of Shrewsbury, in 1627, Penyard passed
to his daughter Elizabeth, Countess of Kent, and it was possessed
by the Partridge family in the 19th century. A farmhouse was built
on part of the site in the late 17th century and there is a record
of 1691 noting a "grant of stone from the demolished castle of
Penyard".

The farmhouse is now very ruined and partly choked by debris
and vegetation, which now also hides the lower parts of a four bay
vaulted undercroft 5m wide and other remains noted by the R.C.H.M.
in the 1930s. The only relics of the castle now visible are a two
light 14th century window re-set into the north gable of the later
house, and now blocked internally, a small fragment of the corner
of a building with walling about 1.2m thick to the west of the
house and its overgrown garden, and traces of ditches further west.
It is likely that the castle had a rectangular courtyard with the
principal apartments overlooking the steep slopes to the south,
and a gatehouse facing the higher ground to the north.

RICHARD'S CASTLE

Richard's Castle is named after Richard Fitz-Scrob, who established a stronghold here in c1050. In 1086, at the time of Domesday Book, the castle was held by his son Osbern Fitz-Richard and was called Avretone (Overton) whilst the adjacent village was called Boiton. Osbern's son Hugh Fitz-Osbern married Eustachia de Say, and whilst their eldest son was known as Osborne Fitz-Hugh, his brother Hugh took the surname de Say, and became lord of Richard's Castle when Osborne died in 1185. Hugh was married to Lucia de Clifford, sister of the famous Rosamund Clifford of Clifford Castle and was probably the builder of the octagonal tower keep at Richard's Castle. The heiress Margaret de Say, their granddaughter, married Robert de Mortimer of Burford. In 1264 the castle was seized for Simon de Montfort. In 1364 Richard's Castle was divided between heiresses who married members of the Cornwall and Talbot families. The latter appear to have inhabited the castle for a while, and Sir Thomas Talbot garrisoned it against Owain Glyndwr, but it was probably little used afterwards. Leland describes it as "going to ruin" and containing just "a poor house of timber in the Castle garth for a farmer". By that time the castle had passed to the Crown and in 1545 Henry VIII granted it to the Earl of Warwick. It was later leased out and since the turn of the 16th and 17th centuries has been held by the Salvey family, who at times have sublet it to the Bradshaws.

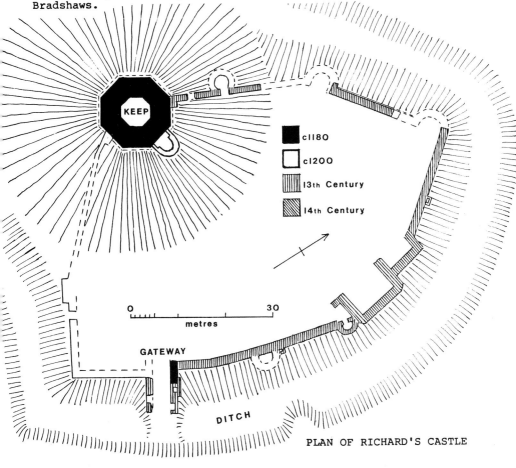

KEEP

■	c1180
□	c1200
▥	13th Century
▨	14th Century

0   30
metres

GATEWAY

DITCH

PLAN OF RICHARD'S CASTLE

The castle lies on a strong commanding site on a hilltop, and comprises a motte with a bailey on the east side, beyond which is the churchyard and the site of the former fortified township. When excavated in 1962-4 the top section of the mound proved to be the earth and debris covered lower storey of an octagonal tower keep of c1185-1200 with an external diameter of 14.5m over walls 4.0m thick. Towards the bailey is a slightly later apsidal projection which may have formed a porch, perhaps with a tiny chapel above. The destroyed inner part of the bailey gatehouse may also have been erected in c1220-40, and the D-shaped towers slightly later. The big rectangular residential tower on the east side was probably added in the 14th century to serve as a solar block for a now-destroyed adjacent hall. The small round tower by the base of the mound on the NW side was converted into a dovecote in the later medieval period when the castle had become no more than a farm. Parts of the NW bailey walls and gatehouse stand high but the rest of the walls are represented only by foundations exposed in the 1960s.

The town may also have had a stone wall and the enclosing bank, which yielded 11th or 12th century pottery, was linked to the wall of the castle bailey by a stone wall in the 13th century. Traces of a 13th century bastion, later converted into a dovecote, were found on the east. Further south is the detached church tower of c1300 set overlooking the approach east of the chancel rather than at the more normal position west of the nave, where it would have hindered defence of the castle. An enquiry of 1364, on the death of Hugh Mortimer, shows that the town then had 103 burgages, and a market and fair were granted to it by King John in 1216. The town subsequently declined and Leland records only two farms and three or four cottages as remaining on the hilltop.

ROSS CASTLE   SO 597243

The Bishops of Hereford had a palace or manor house at Ross. In 1166-7 the Pipe Rolls refer to it being provisioned, and it was then evidently regarded as a defensible structure. It was probably of timber. The cellars of a later medieval house have been found below the Royal Hotel which lies on a good defensive site on the west side of the town close to the medieval-looking round tower and walls of the early 19th century dominating the view here.

Richard's Castle: The bailey wall.

Richard's Castle: The Gatehouse.

SNODHILL CASTLE

It is likely that this motte and bailey castle was constructed in the 1070s or 1080s either by Bernard de Newmarche, or Hugh L'asne, who held this district at the time of Domesday. A Roger de Chandos held it in Henry I's reign. The castle is mentioned in the Roll of Escheats in 1194-7, and in c1200-30 was refortified with a stone keep and bailey walls. When a later Roger de Chandos died in c1355 his castle at Snodhill was surveyed and found to be ruinous. The towers on the bailey wall may be part of a subsequent remodelling.

Sir John Chandos was ordered by Henry IV to fortify the castle against the Welsh in 1403. After Sir John's death in 1428 Snodhill passed to Giles Bruges, but in 1436 was held by Richard de la Mere, sheriff of Herefordshire. It later passed to the Nevilles and seems to have been little used as Leland in c1540 describes it as a ruin. Elizabeth I granted Snodhill to her favourite Robert Dudley, Earl of Leicester, and the estate later passed to the Vaughans. In 1665 they sold it to William Prosser of London, who built or rebuilt Snodhill Court. The old castle had been finally wrecked during the Civil War, having been bombarded by the Scottish army in 1645.

The keep is usually described as a shell keep of an elongated octagonal shape. Yet it measured only 11.5m long by 7m wide within walls 2m thick so it is more likely that it was an unusual form of hall keep with the corners cambered off so as to fit onto the mound summit. The walls were considerably thinner above the offset which carried the floor of the upper storey, making it unlikely that higher levels ever existed. So the building would have had just a hall set above a storage basement. Only two fragments now stand above chest height, showing a narrow basement loop, the jamb of a hall south window, and one side of the entrance with a draw-bar slot behind a door rebate. Later in the 13th century flanking round turrets were added in front of the entrance, with a portcullis between them.

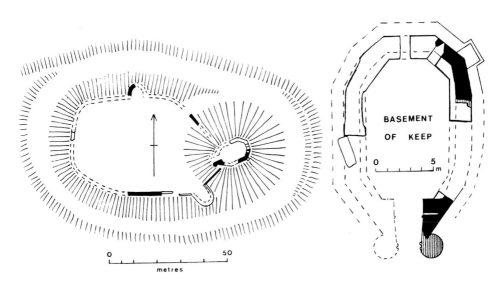

PLANS OF SNODHILL CASTLE

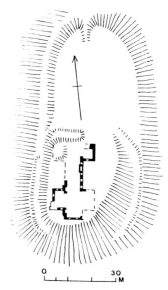

PLAN OF STAPLETON CASTLE

Snodhill Castle

The bailey extends for 60m to the west of the keep and is 40m wide. Part of a curtain wall 2m thick survives to about 1.5m high on the south side, and there are smaller fragments at the west end and on the NE near the mound. On the north side is a high fragment of a round flanking tower which contained octagonal rooms, and at the SW corner is an elongated D-shaped tower or bastion with thin lengths of 14th century walling joining it to the older curtain. It is probable that there were at least two other towers as well.

STAPLETON CASTLE

SO 323656

Stapleton was held by Osbern Fitz-Richard at the time of Domesday and the earthworks may go back to that period. It later passed to the de Says, and is mentioned in 1207 during the minority of Margaret de Say, after which it went by marriage to the Mortimer family of Richard's Castle. In 1304 Stapleton passed to the Cornewalls, and the castle was garrisoned in 1403 against Owain Glyndwr by Sir John Cornewall. In the early 17th century a large H-plan house was built on the motte, the summit of which was probably lowered to receive it and materials from a medieval stone building re-used. The house was thinly walled and ill-equipped for defence but was nevertheless 'defaced' by Sir Michael Woodhouse in 1645 to prevent Parliamentary troops occupying the place. In 1706 the Cornewalls sold Stapleton to the Harleys, who appear to have repaired and re-occupied the house for a while. The house is now very ruined but the south and east walls of the main block and parts of the SW and NE wings still remain. From the house the ground drops considerably to the south and east, but a ditch is provided on the other sides, and on the north an elongated D-shaped bailey platform extends for about 50m.

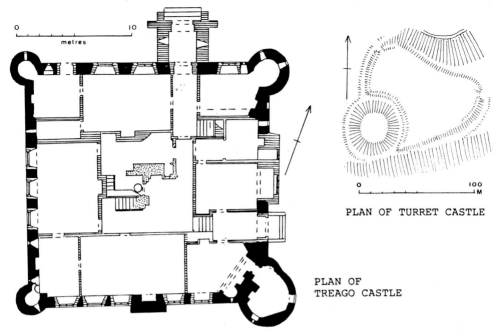

PLAN OF TURRET CASTLE

PLAN OF
TREAGO CASTLE

TREAGO CASTLE

SO 490239

Treago was held by the Mynors family until 1765 when it passed to Peter Rickards on the death of Robert Mynors. John de Mynors may have had a fortified house here in the time of Edward II, but none of the present buildings appear to be older than the end of the 15th century. There are several late medieval type cross-loops in the walls which would appear to be an attempt to make the mansion look older than it actually is. Otherwise, those windows which are not modern are typically Early Tudor with square heads and lights with four-centered arches. The site is a shelf commanded by rising ground to the west and it is assumed there was once a wet moat.

The house is roughly a square of about 20m with outside walls 1m thick. There were thinly walled ranges of rooms set around a court 7.6m square. Originally the kitchen lay in the south range and the entrance was in the middle of the east range where there is a much rebuilt shallow projection. Probably the hall lay in the west range, although one description of the castle says that it was in the north range. Round turrets formerly containing spiral stairs, and measuring about 2.6m in external diameter, project from the two western corners, whilst the NE and SE corners have larger turrets of 3.7m and 5.0m external diameter respectively containing rooms. All the turrets rise one level above the two storeys of the main ranges, and are covered with conical roofs. The SE tower had a spiral stair built into the junction with the south wall and has a projecting topmost storey which was built in the late 18th century for Charles Morgan. The existing doorway in the east range is mid 16th century, and of the same period is the present main entrance in the north front with a buttressed three storey porch. The roofs of the ranges are mostly of the late 16th century whilst the upper rooms were much altered in the 17th century. The castle fell into decay when let out as a farm in the early 19th century. Alterations made during the restoration of the 1840s included filling in the courtyard to provide a central hall and stairs, etc.

TREGATE CASTLE   SO 480171

Above the River Monnow is a large motte 3.5m high with a rampart
on top covering the footings of stone curtain walling. There are
signs of outer enclosures which have been damaged by the erection
of farm buildings.

TRETIRE CASTLE   SO 521238

South of a house by the church is a platform with on the north side
a ditch and rampart. The latter may conceal remnants of a curtain
wall with several towers built by Fulke Fitz-Warine, lord of the
Shropshire castles of Whittington and Alberbury, in the early 13th
century. Foundations were traced in the 19th century. In 1292 there
was a dispute over possession of the castle between John Tregoz and
Walter de Huntley.

TURRET CASTLE   SO 259534

This earthwork is likely to be the site of the original fortress
of the lordship of Huntingdon later superseded by the site north
of the church. By the end of a steep sided spur is a large kidney
shaped bailey with a rampart and ditch, and having a small outer
court to the east on the end of the spur, and a motte 9m high with
a summit 24m across defending it from higher ground to the west.

URISHAY CASTLE   SO 323376

Urishay was held by the de la Hays under the Mortimer and Chandos
families. A mound rises 6m from its ditch to a summit about 30m
in diameter which was perhaps lowered when a large house was built
on it in the 17th century. The house may incorporate older material
and has only fallen into ruin during this century as a drawing of
1865 still shows it inhabitable and with the walls not roughcasted
as they are at present.

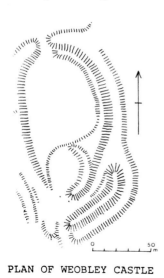

PLAN OF WEOBLEY CASTLE

Urishay Castle

Weobley Castle

WEOBLEY CASTLE

SO 403513

This castle was built by the de Lacys soon after the Conquest. It was fortified by Geoffrey Talbot against King Stephen, who in 1138 besieged and captured it. In 1208-9 the castle was used as a base by William de Braose during his rebellion against King John, and from it he sallied out to burn the town of Leominster. It was then a possession of Walter de Lacy, who had wide possessions in Ireland and the Welsh Marches, and had married Matilda de Braose in c1200. Walter was all-powerful in Herefordshire in the period 1216-1223, when he was sheriff of the county and responsible for its defence against the Welsh. It is almost certain that the now-vanished walls and towers at Weobley were constructed in that period. Walter's son Gilbert and grandson Walter died before his own death in 1241, at which Weobley passed to his daughter Margaret, who married John de Verdon. In 1388 Weobley passed to the Devereux family who became Earls of Essex in Elizabeth I's reign. The last Earl died in 1646 and Weobley passed by marriage to the Dukes of Somerset and then later to the Thynne family. Leland describes the castle as decayed and it was probably little used during the 16th and 17th centuries.

The castle earthworks lie on flat ground at the south end of the village. They comprise a ringwork with an oval bailey measuring 75m long by 65m wide to the north, and a strong outer bank to the south, the whole being surrounded by moats which were probably once water filled. The ringwork is very badly damaged but the eastern part may survive to about the full original height. It measured about 30m across at the top of the rampart. The bailey still has an impressive rampart on the east side, probably with foundations buried within it, but any rampart that once existed on the west side has now vanished.

A very interesting plan of the stone buildings made in 1655 by Silas Taylor has survived. It is evidently diagrammatical rather than an accurate survey, but is indicates that there were six round towers flanking the outer walls, a gateway at the north end, and on or within the ringwork was a rectangular tower keep with round corner towers. This keep was probably a 13th century structure and may either have been built by Walter de Lacy or his successors the Verdons. There are several 13th century keeps on this plan still surviving in Ireland, but the earliest structures of this type in England and Wales are those of c1310-20 and c1348-60 respectively on the mottes at Dudley and Stafford. The plan also shows a pair of purely domestic buildings standing north of the keep.

45

WHITNEY CASTLE

This castle was the seat of the Whitney family who were descended from Turstin the Fleming, who held land here in Henry I's reign. In 1675 the existence of a former stone tower was still remembered by locals. The site was destroyed in 1730 when the Wye changed course.

WIGMORE CASTLE

Wigmore was one of the castles founded by William Fitz-Osbern in 1067-70. After the forfeiture of his son Roger de Breteuil in 1075 it was granted to Ralph Mortimer and became the chief seat of his descendants until the male line ended with Edmund Mortimer in 1425. The castle was captured by Henry II's forces from Hugh de Mortimer in 1155, and forces loyal to Richard I captured it from his son Roger when he supported Prince John's rebellion in 1191. In 1264 Roger de Mortimer III supported Henry III, and Wigmore Castle was probably attacked by Simon de Montfort's forces. However, it was evidently in Mortimer hands in May 1265, when Prince Edward sought refuge at the castle after his escape from Hereford.

The castle must have possessed stone defences by the time of the 1191 siege but they were mostly rebuilt by Roger de Mortimer IV in the early 14th century. Roger joined the Bohun Earl of Hereford and other Marcher lords in opposition to the Despencers, favourites of Edward II. In 1322 he was forced to submit to Edward and was imprisoned in the Tower of London. With the assistance of Bishop Orleton of Hereford he escaped and fled to France where he became the ally and lover of Edward's estranged queen, Isabella. In 1326 they returned to England, deposed Edward II, and ruled in the name of the young Edward III until 1330, when the latter arrested Roger at Nottingham Castle, and promptly had him executed for treason. Wigmore was granted to William Montacute, Earl of Salisbury, and Roger de Mortimer V only regained his father's estates and Earldom of March, created in 1328, by marrying Montacute's heiress in 1354.

In 1425 Wigmore and the Earldom of March passed to Richard, Duke of York, a great-grandson of Edward III, and the son of the heiress Anne Mortimer. Richard became involved in a power struggle against the weak Henry VI and the Beaufort Dukes of Somerset. He was killed at the Battle of Wakefield in December 1460, but his son won a notable victory at Mortimer's Cross near Wigmore in February 1461, and then seized the throne as Edward IV. By this time Wigmore Castle had been eclipsed in importance by that of Ludlow nearby. However, it was still inhabited in 1579, when Sir Robert Harley, the noted Parliamentarian, was born within it, and in 1642 the Harleys dismantled the fortfications to prevent their use by the Royalists.

The gateway,
Wigmore Castle.

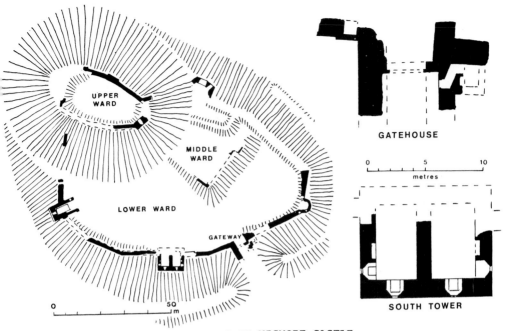

UPPER WARD

MIDDLE WARD

LOWER WARD

GATEWAY

0   50
         m

GATEHOUSE

0   5   10
      metres

SOUTH TOWER

PLANS OF WIGMORE CASTLE

The castle is impressively and strongly sited on a ridge. The large motte faces the higher ground to the NW from which it is separated by a very deep ditch. There is a square platform below the motte to the east which may have borne the principal domestic buildings, and to the east and south is a spacious bailey over a 100m long from east to west, with a ditch, and outer bank to the SE, facing the approach. Partly visible from afar and partly hidden amongst the dense vegetation covering the site are considerable fragments of the shell keep and bailey walls. Although breached in several places most of the walls around the south and east sides of the bailey still remain, and foundations of the other sections must survive under the soil and debris. On the north side, close to the motte, is the outer half of an irregularly polygonal tower. The D-shaped east tower with an external diameter of about 5.5m is thought to be 13th century work. Facing the approach are remains of a rectangular gatehouse, probably once of three storeys. It is 8.4m wide but the inner and outer ends have vanished so that the length cannot be determined. A half buried arch remains which lay halfway along the entrance passage. The passage in the east wall at the level of the room above led to a latrine projection. The rectangular south tower contained two pairs of pleasant living rooms set over two vaulted cellars. The tower is 11.8m long by 8.8m wide and was similar to a contemporary tower added to Ludlow Castle. It has single light windows in wide embrasures with seats, and traces of a latrine on the wall adjoining to the west. The SW tower was a long narrow rectangular structure with two single rooms set over a dark basement. As with the south tower the outer parts stand high but the inner portions are mostly destroyed down to ground level.

The North Tower, Wigmore Castle.

The East Tower,
Wilton Castle

On the mound summit are the remains of walls over 2m thick enclosing a court 20m wide by nearly 40m long. Much of the north wall still stands 7m high, and has a shallow projecting turret in the middle. To the SE is a similar projecting turret with a window embrasure in it, and between the two fragments must have lain the gateway. Only foundations remain of the south wall, whilst to the west is a high fragment of a stair turret which appears to have served a tower keep or high range of apartments occupying the whole of this end. Probably walling of this structure still survives several metres high underneath the mound of soil and debris around the turret fragment.

WILTON CASTLE

SO 590244

The site of this castle was of strategic importance as it guarded one of the very few bridges over the Wye. There are indications of a former motte and bailey below the present stonework, and this stronghold is mentioned by Giraldus Cambrensis and in the Pipe Rolls for 1188 and 1204-6. It was then held by Hugh Longchamp, and later passed to William Fitz-Hugh, and then by marriage to Roger de Grey who rebuilt the castle in stone at the end of the 13th century. It probably fell into decay in the 15th century and in the late 16th century was partly replaced by a new house built by the Brydges family. Sir John Brydges, who died in 1651, remained neutral in the Civil War, but, although there is evidence that the castle was not regarded as tenable as a fortress by Parliament, it was burnt by Barnaby Scudamore to prevent it being garrisoned. The ruins were sold in 1722 to Guy's Hospital in London, but in 1784 the ancient title Lord Grey of Wilton was revived and granted to Sir Thomas Egerton, and an Earldom of Wilton was created in 1801. In the 19th century parts of the ruin were patched up and extended to make a new residence which is still inhabited.

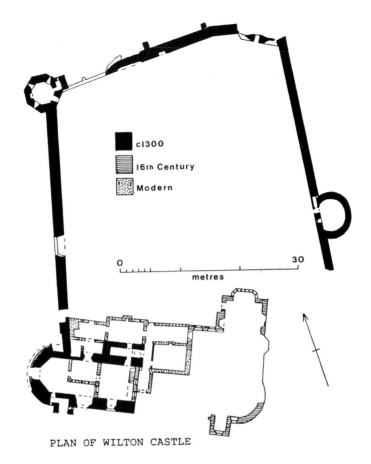

PLAN OF WILTON CASTLE

The original motte probably lay at the SE corner, commanding the bridge, which in its present form is of the late 16th century. The defensive walls around this section have vanished but close by are ruins of the Elizabethan mansion. The layout of the rooms is now difficult to discern. The curtain walls still stand high around the east, west and northern sides, although the latter is breached by the NW tower, with the remainder buttressed outside. The eastern tower is semi-circular and about 7.6m in external diameter. It is now very cracked and damaged. Beside its entrance doorway is a latrine in the thickness of the wall. The NW tower is octagonal and is about 6m in external diameter. It has a projection beside where it joins the north curtain to contain latrines. The NE tower has been destroyed except for a part of the straight side facing the courtyard. This suggests it was circular or polygonal, and larger than the east and NW towers. The SW tower is 10m wide and measures 14m long from the straight east wall to the rounded western end. There is a projection from the east half of the north side and a small latrine projection from the western part of the south side. It is assumed that the gateway was through or adjacent to this tower but the precise arrangement is now unknown. The western part of the tower is ruinous, and the eastern part has been incorporated into the Elizabethan house, and into the existing inhabited house.

49

MINOR NORMAN EARTHWORKS IN HEREFORDSHIRE

BACTON (SO 371335) A tiny mound lies in the eastern part of a pear shaped bailey with a rampart and ditch on the flatter west side.

BAGE (SO 298433) The small mound is now very defaced.

BRILLEY (SO 276514) North of Cwmna farm is a mound 5m high with a ditch on its western side.

BUCKTON (SO 383732) A small defaced mound 4m high lies beside the Teme, SW of the village. Two smaller oval mounds, one 3m high, lie 1.5km to the north (SO 393740).

CABAL (SO 345585) A moated mound lies 2.5km NE of Lyonshall Castle.

CASTLE TWTS (SO 276555) A low mound with a bailey facing the higher ground to the north looks out over the Arrow 2km SW of Kington.

CHANSTONE (SO 366359) This mound beside a stream near Vowchurch is 4.5m high and has a summit diameter of about 28m. A second mound nearby is oval and about 1.2m high.

COMBE (SO 348635) A mound 2.5m high lies by the Hindwell Brook near where it joins the River Lugg.

DIDLEY (SO 451320) Farm buildings occupy the small bailey to the NW of a damaged mound 5.5m high overlooking a drop to the east.

DILWYN (SO 416544) A ringwork or moated site lies south of Dilwyn.

HEREFORDSHIRE BEACON (SO 760401) 12th century pottery has been dug up in the ringwork which crowns the top of the hill within the Iron Age hillfort.

HOW CAPLE (SO 613306) A mound 3.5m high lies SE of the church.

KING'S CAPLE (SO 559288) A small mound lies south of the church.

KINSHAM (SO 362645 and 358646) A 2m high mound lies 1km SSW of the church, near the river. Another, 1.2m high, lies 300m to the WNW.

LAYSTERS (SO 568632) South of the church is a mound 3m high with a summit diameter of 24m.

LEMORE (SO 310517) The moat 2km north of Eardisley may be the site of the "domus defensabilis" recorded at Ailey in Domesday Book.

LITTLE HEREFORD (SO 554679) The de la Mares' seat is represented by a triangular bailey between the church and the Teme, with at the west corner a worn down motte now only 1.5m high.

LOWER PEDWARDINE (SO 368705) A small damaged mound rising up to 3m. At Upper Pedwardine (SO 365707) is a second damaged mound.

LYE (SO 396654) A substantial ringwork overlooks the River Lugg.

MADLEY (SO 406384) Traces of a motte and bailey lie to the NW of the church.

MANSELL LACY (SO 426455) SE of the church is a moated mound.

MICHAELCHURCH ESCLEY (SO 296356) The oval ringwork measures about 28m across from north to south and has a feint bailey platform.

MONNINGTON COURT (SO 382368) A mound 3.5m high lies by the farm.

MUCH DEWCHURCH (SO 485312) An overgrown oval ringwork 60m across with a bailey platform to the west lies NE of the church.

MUNSLEY (SO 661409) A house now lies on the lowered motte. Two arms of a wet moat around a bailey to the west still remain.

MYNYDDBRYDD (SO 280415 & 278410) A motte 5.5m high with a bailey to the west lies SW of the farm. A second mound lies on the hillside to the SW at Nant-Y-Bar.

OLDCASTLE TWT (SO 328520) The damaged mound 5.5m high with a summit diameter of 9m, and its bailey to the north, lie on a spur end.

ROWLSTONE (SO 375272) A mound 5m high and bailey NE of the church.

ST MARGARET'S (SO 360340) The mound 600m ENE of the church varies from 1.5m to 3m high and is damaged on the SE side.

SHOBDON (SO 399628) A mound 3m high lies 125m west of the church, and another mound 3m high lies 250m to the south of the church.

SOLLERS HOPE (SO 613333) North of the church is a low moated mound.

STAUNTON ON ARROW (SO 369000) West of the church is a mound rising 8m to a summit 19m across. Traces of a bailey lie to the SW.

TURNASTONE (SO 339363) High on the hillside 2km west of the village is a small damaged motte 3.5m high.

TURRET TUMP (SO 246521) A mound 5m high lies high up on a knoll 1km south of Huntingdon church.

WACTON (SO 614575) North of the Court is a small mound 3.5m high.

WALFORD (SO 391724) The mound lies in former marshland between two tributaries of the River Teme.

WALTERSTONE (SO 339250) West of the church is a 9m high mound with the southern part of its ditch still full of water. To the east, NE, and south are traces of bailey platforms.

WOODBROOK (SO 304544) This feeble motte and bailey lies 2.5km south of Kington.

Chanstone Motte, near Vowchurch.

MOATED SITES IN HEREFORDSHIRE

BIRCHEND SO 666447 A moat lies close to the house
BISHOPSTONE SO 416440 Stone lined rectangular moat west of Court.
BODENHAM SO 528510 The Devereux seat at Moat House was moated.
BOSBURY SO 695436 Traces of a moat west of Old Court Farm.
BREDWARDINE SO 336449 Traces of moat by Old Court near bridge.
BRINSOP SO 446458 Wet moat at Court. Two other moats lie nearby.
BROCKBURY SO 746419 Part of a triangular moat north of the house.
BROCKHAMPTON SO 688560 Wet moat around old timber framed house.
BRYNGWYN SO 484306 Rectangular wet moat beside a farm track.
BURGHILL SO 478445 A moat west of the church is now filled in.
CLOUDS SO 592381 Earthwork in plantation near stream.
COURT OF NOKE SO 372595 There are slight traces of a moat.
COURT-Y-PARK SO 646397 House on mound. Slight evidence of moat.
CUMMIN'S FARM SO 738410 Part of moat remains north of the house.
DONNINGTON SO 708342 Moat south of church is still partly wet.
EDWYN RALPH SO 644575 Round moat and outer enclosures by church.
FORD SO 564585 Part of square moat remains south of the house.
FREETOWN SO 635420 Part of a wet moat survives by the farm.
GILLOW MANOR SO 532254 The 14th century house was formerly moated.
HELL MOAT SO 366520 Dry earthwork in woodland.
HINTON SO 574473 Pool by farm is a moat with the platform removed.
HOPE MANSELL SO 624199 Slight traces of moat around Moat Farm.
HOPTON SO 668471 One dry arm of wide moat north of the farmhouse.
KINSHAM SO 362645 Moat around Lower Court House nearly filled in.
LANGSTONE COURT SO 536219 Rectangular wet moat SE of the Court.
LEOMINSTER SO 496584 A rectangular moat lay 750m south of church.
LITTLE SARNESFIELD SO 388522 Rectangular moat. Causeway on north.
LORD'S WOOD SO 555150 Triangular moat 2km south of Whitchurch.
LOWER HOPTON SO 632493 Circular moat near the farmhouse.
LUGWARDINE SO 550413 Large dry moat not far north of the church.
MADLEY SO 416386 Fragment of a moat 350m west of the church.
MAINSTONE COURT SO 658398 Irregular platform within wide wet moat.
MANSELL LACY SO 426455 Platform 1.2m high with partly wet moat.
MARTIN'S CASTLE SO 649604 Rectangular moat.
MEER COURT SO 438364 Part of a wet moat remains SW of the Court.
MOOR ABBEY SO 545633 Fragment of moat by house. Fishpond beyond.
MOREHAMPTON PARK SO 377341 Traces of former moat around the farm.
MORETON ON LUGG SO 504456 South and west arms remain of a wet moat.
NEW HOUSE SO 645445 One arm of a moat remains to the SE of house.
NUNSLAND SO 379538 Wet moat SE of house. NW side is obliterated.
OLDCASTLE SO 754407 Platform has now been removed from wet moat.
PAUNCEFORD COURT SO 674406 The dry east arm of the moat remains.
PEMBRIDGE SO 391580 Dry moat south of church. Pembridge family seat.
RUSHALL SO 642348 An oval moat has now been obliterated.
ST DEVEREUX SO 439302 Square moat now mostly filled in.
SHOWLE COURT SO 612437 Fragment of wet moat to south of house.
SHUCKNALL SO 587424 Only a small pool survives of the moat.
STOKE LACY SO 620493 Two arms remain of a wet moat near a house.
TARRINGTON SO 616405 A fragment of a moat survives at the Court.
TEMPLE COURT SO 691433 This Templar preceptory was once moated.
TRELOUGH SO 432312 The moat around the house is mostly filled in.
ULLINGSWICK SO 590495 A square moat lies 700m WSW of the church.
UPLEADEON SO 668419 Slight traces of a moat remain in an orchard.
WACTON SO 616575 Slight traces of a former moat around the Court.
WALSOPTHORNE SO 650424 Only fragments now remain of the moat.
WETTON SO 373537 The pool is a relic of a former moat.
WHITBOURNE SO 726568 Oval moat around house. Filled in on NW side.
YARKHILL SO 608425 Rectangular moat with very overgrown platform.

MAP OF CASTLES IN HEREFORDSHIRE

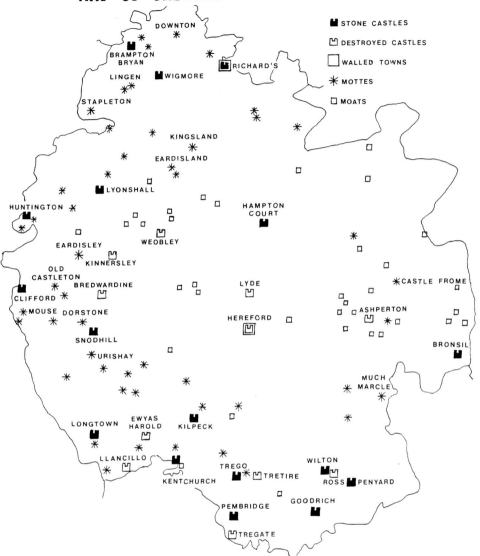

STONE CASTLES

DESTROYED CASTLES

WALLED TOWNS

MOTTES

MOATS

DOWNTON

BRAMPTON BRYAN

LINGEN WIGMORE

STAPLETON

RICHARD'S

KINGSLAND

EARDISLAND

LYONSHALL

HUNTINGTON

HAMPTON COURT

EARDISLEY

WEOBLEY

KINNERSLEY

OLD CASTLETON

BREDWARDINE

LYDE

CASTLE FROME

CLIFFORD

MOUSE DORSTONE

HEREFORD

ASHPERTON

SNODHILL

URISHAY

BRONSIL

MUCH MARCLE

LONGTOWN

EWYAS HAROLD

KILPECK

LLANCILLO

KENTCHURCH

TREGO

TRETIRE

WILTON

ROSS PENYARD

PEMBRIDGE

GOODRICH

TREGATE

PUBLIC ACCESS TO THE CASTLES AND EARTHWORKS

Free access at any time. Some of these are upon private land. Obey the Country Code. Hereford, Kilpeck, Longtown, Penyard, Elmley, Richard's, Snodhill, Weobley, Wigmore.

Fee Payable: Croft, Goodrich, Hartlebury.

Viewable from public roads: Almeley, Clifford, Castlemorton, Holt.

Many other earthworks and ruins can be reached or viewed from paths or tracks which are rights of way on foot. For those in private fields and woods ask permission first.

INTRODUCTION TO THE CASTLES OF WORCESTERSHIRE

Worcestershire has one of the lowest concentrations of castles in England, although there are plenty of the ordinary domestic moated sites, with good examples at Harvington Hall, Throckmorton, Earl's Croome, and Astwood Court. The county lies far from any contentious or raidable coast or border and an unusually high proportion of the manors within it were held by the four great monastic houses of Worcester, Evesham, Pershore, and Malvern. Some of their granges were moated, as were some of the manor houses of the Bishops of Worcester. Only at Hartlebury did the Bishops have a proper castle having a quadrangular courtyard with a gatehouse, corner towers, and many fine apartments, although their palace at Worcester was also a licensed embattled building.

A royal motte and bailey castle was raised at Worcester soon after the Norman Conquest, and was partly refortified in stone in John's reign, only to be dismantled early in Henry III's reign. John built a fortified hunting lodge at Hanley which later passed to the de Clares and le Despencers before being dismantled for its materials in Henry VIII's reign.

From the early 12th century until the mid 15th century the principal baronial family in the county was the Beauchamps. They had a substantial castle at Elmley with a rectangular tower keep standing within a large stone walled bailey, but from the mid 13th century onwards they preferred the more accessible Warwick Castle, and Elmley was left to decay. The Beauchamps briefly also had a castle at Bengeworth, and in the 1380s another branch of the family built an embattled house at Holt. The only other baronial castles were the motte and bailey strongholds at Castlemorton, Ham, and Leigh, a castle of uncertain date and form at Beoley, and the fortified houses at Inkberrow and Strensham, of which only the moats remain.

Hartlebury became the principal castle in Worcestershire after the demise of Worcester castle and Elmley's eclipse by Warwick. It and Strensham Castle were both held for the King in the Civil War and their walls and towers were mostly demolished afterwards. Much altered domestic apartments and moats remain at Hartlebury. Elmley has considerable earthworks and buried foundations, and a single tower remains at Holt. The de Somery castles of Dudley and Weoley, once within Worcestershire, but now in the West Midlands County, are described in an earlier volume in this series.

Hartlebury Castle

GAZETTEER OF CASTLES IN WORCESTERSHIRE

ALVECHURCH MOAT
SP 032726

The site of the manor house of the Bishops of Worcester is now only represented by two adjacent moated platforms set above gullies in which run the River Arrow and a tributary stream. One platform is roughly 54m square and is still entirely surrounded by water held in by a strong outer bank to the SW and SE. The other platform is the same width and extends for about 80m to the NE. A house lies in the NE corner of the latter, where the moat has been filled in. Leland describes the house as being a timber structure of recent origin which had just been repaired by Bishop Latimer. The form of the building in which Bishop Blois died in 1236, and which was much used by Bishop Giffard, is uncertain. It may never have been built of stone. Parliament sold the house in 1648, but it was restored to the bishops in the 1660s. The house was destroyed by 1780 and in 1860 the see gave the site to the Ecclesiastical Commissioners.

BENGEWORTH CASTLE
SP 041437

Bengeworth was held by Urse D'Abitot at the time of Domesday but it appears to have been his successors the Beauchamps who raised a castle here beside the bridge over the River Severn in the reign of King Stephen. During those lawless years Walter de Beauchamp raided nearby Evesham Abbey, for which he was excommunicated, and the forces of Abbot William de Andeville occupied and then destroyed the castle, and created a cemetery on the site. The Beauchamps gave the site to the Abbey in 1268. The moat was still traceable in the 19th century.

BEOLEY CASTLE
SP 066694

A spur commanding an extensive view has a ditch around the summit creating a quite strongly defended oval area measuring over 100m from SW to NE by 85m wide. This may be the site of the Beauchamps' house accidentally burnt down in 1303, but replaced by 1316 when a court and grange are recorded as existing.

CASTLEMORTON MOTTE
SO 795371

South of the church is an oval mound about 6m high standing in the southern half of a bailey. The castle appears to have been built in King Stephen's reign by the Folliotts. They sold Castlemorton to Richard de Berking, Abbot of Westminster from 1222 to 1246, who is recorded as having a chapel and chaplain there. The castle is last heard of in Edward I's reign.

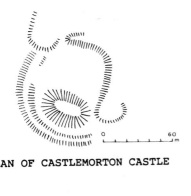

PLAN OF CASTLEMORTON CASTLE

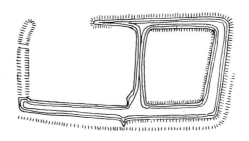

PLAN OF ALVECHURCH MOAT

ELMLEY CASTLE

Shortly after the time of the Domesday survey of 1086 a castle was built at Elmley by Robert D'Abitot. He being childless, the castle passed to his brother Urso, hereditary sheriff of Worcestershire. Urso's son Roger was disinherited for slaying a royal messenger and Elmley passed through his daughter Emmeline to her husband Walter de Beauchamp. His son William was in possession during the wars of Stephen's reign, during which the castle was probably strengthened.

In 1234 Walter Beauchamp enclosed a park below the castle and stocked it with 10 does and 3 bucks donated by Henry III. Elmley was then the foremost castle in Worcestershire, having superseded that at Worcester. However, William Beauchamp, who died in 1269, married Isabel, the sister and heiress of William Mauduit, Earl of Warwick, and in 1267 their son William inherited the Earldom and castle of Warwick. The latter was more conveniently sited than the hilltop stronghold at Elmley, and quickly became the family seat. Elmley Castle was left to decay and when surveyed in 1316 was so out of repair that it was regarded as worth nothing. Minor repairs appear to have been effected later but a memoranda of 1540 says that "the late Castle of Elmley standing on high.....adjoining the Park compassed in with wall and ditch is uncovered and in decay". Leland in the same period saw only one tower left standing and saw stone from the castle being carted off to repair Pershore Bridge.

The castle was built within the eastern portion of an Iron Age hillfort set on a strong and commanding site high up on the north side of Bredon Hill. The castle has high ramparts and deep ditches around a pear shaped area 150m long from north to south by 100m wide. The base of a stone curtain wall about 1.6m thick around the castle is exposed on the north, and lies within the rampart on the south. In the middle is part of what may be the base of the keep, or, to be more precise, the forebuilding or porch which protected the side containing the entrance. This keep may have lain on the line of a wall dividing the bailey into two, with the northern end forming the inner court. In the 13th century there would have been extensive domestic buildings and outbuildings. Some excavations were carried out in the 1930s but no report was ever published.

Elmley Castle

HAM CASTLE
SO 735619

Immediately north of the farmhouse of Homme Castle, and on a spur
within a wide bend of the River Teme is a worn down motte about 3m
high which is mentioned in 1207. Amongst the farmhouse outbuildings
is a long brick vaulted cellar of the 17th or 18th century.

HANLEY CASTLE
SO 838414

Hanley Castle was built in 1207-12 by King John as a hunting lodge
at a cost of nearly £750. He was there in 1209 and 1213, and assizes
were held at the castle in 1211-12. Henry III granted the castle
to Gilbert de Clare early in his reign. After the last Gilbert de
Clare was killed at the Battle of Bannockburn in 1314 the castle
passed via his heiress Eleanor to her husband Hugh le Despencer.
In 1321-2 Hanley Castle was damaged by the rebel barons who hated
the favoured Despencers. Hugh was executed in 1326, and the Earl
of March briefly had possession in 1330, but it was returned to the
widowed Eleanor de Clare, who was still living at Hanley Castle in
c1349, when extensions to the apartments were supposedly made. In
1416, Eleanor, widow of Richard le Despencer, was granted the use of
the following parts of the castle.."a great room at the end of the
wall to the west with two towers of stone annex'd the said hall
with one third of the pantry and buttery under the said room...two
rooms called les guesten chambres, three towers in the south of the
castle with a fourth tower in the corner of the castle towards the
south,..a third of the bakehouse and kitchen adjacent to said tower
.....with a third of the pallisade and moat around the castle". She
also had use of the chapel, and a third of the garden of the manor
and a third of the park, but had to pay a third of the constable's
fees. The castle was evidently then an extensive residence.
    Hanley Castle later passed by marriage to the Earls of Warwick.
Repairs to the chapel, mill, kitchen, gatehouse, and drawbridge are
recorded in the 1480s. Henry VII had the young new Earl of Warwick
executed in 1499 as a dangerous rival, and then retained the castle,
giving custody of it to Sir John Savage. In Henry VIII's reign the
custodian was Sir William Crompton, who dismantled the building for
its materials. Leland refers to him as having "clene defacid it yn
his tyme".

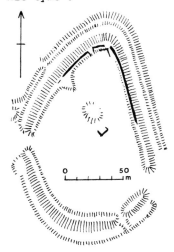

PLAN OF ELMLEY CASTLE

PLAN OF HANLEY CASTLE

Hartlebury Castle

Later in the 16th century Hanley Castle was owned by Roland Badger. Although Habington in the 17th century commented that the 'castell is so vanished as theare appearethe nothinge in that place but a littel rubbyshe and a silly barne", and the Badgers lived at Pool House, one of the castle towers stood until 1795, when it was pulled down by the then owner Thomas Hornyold to provide materials for repairing the bridge at Upton on Severn. Prior to this a house was built on part of the castle site. It was destroyed by fire in 1904 and has now itself vanished. In 1884 Mrs Lawson described how a considerable extent of the footings of the castle outer wall 2.7m thick had been exposed, unfortunately without any plan being made. An oven was also then visible, and a number of domestic artifacts were found. All that now remains is a dry moat around a platform.

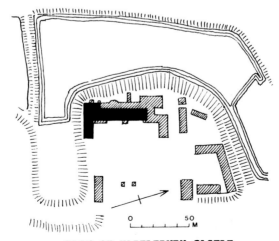

0   50
L_I_I_I_I_I
M

PLAN OF HARTLEBURY CASTLE

HARTLEBURY CASTLE

Hartlebury was given to the Bishops of Worcester by Burghred, King of Mercia. In the 1250s Bishop Walter de Cantilupe had a moat dug around the manor house, and in 1268 King Henry III licensed Bishop Giffard to build embattled curtain walls and towers. Thus laid out with a quadrangular courtyard with corner towers, a gatehouse in the middle of the east side, and a wide wet moat, the castle would have been a scaled down version of some of Edward I's castles in North Wales, and similar to the less strong contemporary castles of Caverswall and Eccleshall in Staffordshire, the latter a house of the Bishops of Lichfield. Bishop Giffard entertained Edward I at Hartlebury in 1282, and provided military forces for the King's expedition in North Wales which culminated in the Welsh defeat.

In the mid 15th century Bishop Carpenter built a new gatehouse and drawbridge on the east side. Possibly this was the 'keep', the last vestiges of which were removed by Bishop Hurd in 1781, although there are no signs of it on the Buck brothers' engraving of 1731, which shows the east side much as it is now, with gateway pavilions. Much of the walling of the great hall and the saloon at its south end also probably dates from the time of Bishop Carpenter, whilst the chapel, although much altered, may date from the last years of the 13th century. In c1540 Leland described the castle as a "fayre Maner Place....having ii lyttel towers covered with leade, and the chamber cauled the Bishop's Chamber also covered with Leade, and there is a Chappell annexed to the said Chamber lykewyse covered with Leade, where is a lytell Bell weying by estimacion dimid hundred Weight. Also there is a Mote and a Ponde adjoyning to the said castell well stored with fyshe". About this time the castle became the principal residence of the Bishops. It became their sole residence in 1846.

In 1644 King Charles' Commissioners of Array took refuge at the castle when pursued by Parliamentary forces. In 1646 William Sandys fortified the castle for the King, installing a garrison of 120 foot and 20 horse with provisions to last twelve months. In May of that year the castle was surrendered to Colonel Thomas Morgan after a two day siege. In 1647 the castle was sold to Thomas Westrowe for £3,133.6s.6d. and in 1648 it was used as a prison for incarcerating Royalist plotters. A survey then described it as a "stong castle situate upon a rock, with a moate around it full of water, which filleth several ponds stored with fish.." which suggests the walls were then still complete, but at some point during this period the defensive walls and towers were dismantled.

The castle was eventually restored to the Bishops, and in 1675 Bishop Fleetwood began rebuilding the domestic apartments. Of this period are the whole of the NE wing, the central porch, the long gallery on the west side, and many windows and fireplaces serving the older rooms. In 1745 Bishop Maddox spent £1,200 on remodelling the chapel. It was provided with a pretty fan vault designed by the architect Henry Keene, and a new set of windows with Y-tracery. Further work was carried out to the other rooms in c1750-9, and the central lantern added, while between 1759 and 1774 Bishop Johnson refurnished the saloon and provided it with new gothic windows. In the 1780s Bishop Hurd had a library built over the long gallery, and a westward facing bow window added.

In 1905-18 Bishop Yeatman Biggs turned the stable block into a college for clergy, and in 1964 the north wing and adjoining rooms were taken over by Worcestershire County Council and converted into the County Museum, which is open daily.

HOLT CASTLE

Holt was held by Urse D'Abitot at the time of Domesday, and passed with his daughter to the Beauchamps. William Beauchamp in the mid 13th century gave Holt to his younger son John, and it is likely that a new manor house was built in that period. The oldest part of the existing building is a 14th century tower which is a relic of a house built by John Beauchamp, who was knighted and granted an estate in North Wales in 1385. He was created Lord Beauchamp of Kidderminster in 1387, and, being one of Richard II's unpopular favourites, was executed by the Lords Appellants in 1388, and his honours forfeited. They were later restored to his son John, but were forfeited again after Henry IV's accession in 1399.

Holt passed to the Guise family in 1472, and was sold in 1557 to Sir John Bourn. He in turn sold it to Thomas Fortescue in 1578 and it was settled on his daughter Elizabeth and her husband Sir Thomas Bromley, then Lord Chancellor. The Croft family also had a part of the manor, but the whole was re-united under Henry Bromley, who died in 1615. Another Henry Bromley was made Lord Montfort in 1741. He sold Holt in c1760 to Thomas, Lord Foley, later Earl of Dudley, and it has remained subsequently with the Dudley family.

The four storey tower measuring 7.0m by 7.7m externally was probably one of four standing at the corners of a rectangular main block, as at Broncroft Castle in Shropshire, built by Sir Simon Burley, another of Richard II's favourites executed in 1388, and the earlier house at Acton Burnell, also in Shropshire. Like these buildings the house at Holt would have been embattled, and perhaps was surrounded by a wet moat, now filled in, but the walls would have been thin and pierced with large windows, with defence taking much the second place to comfort. The whole building may never have been fully completed, for in the 15th century a new hall, probably on more modest lines than the original, was built against the tower, in the basement of which an entrance passage was then made. North of the hall is a contemporary solar block which retains a number of original features, notably parts of the roof, although considerable further additions and alterations were made in the 16th and 18th centuries. In the latter period a service wing at the south end was removed.

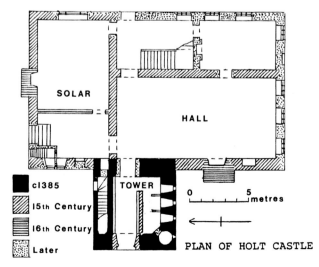

SOLAR

HALL

c1385
15th Century
16th Century
Later

TOWER

0   5 metres

PLAN OF HOLT CASTLE

Holt Castle

INKBERROW CASTLE   SP 017573

John Marshall, who died in c1193, or his brother William, Earl of
Pembroke, built a castle or fortified manor house at Inkberrow. In
1216 the Crown ordered William Cauntelow to provide wood to repair
it, and in 1231 King John's daughter Eleanor, widow of the second
William Marshall, Earl of Pembroke, was allowed to reside in the
castle, but in 1233, during the revolt of Richard Marshall, it was
confiscated by Henry III, given to Baldwin de Lisle, and then later
in the year destroyed by the sheriff of Worcester. Inkberrow was
later restored to Richard's brother Gilbert, who restocked the park
there in 1234, and was evidently building a residence in 1235. The
house passed by marriage to the Monchelseys in 1241, and on their
forfeiture in 1265 went to William de Valence. From 1310 to 1389
it was held by the Hastings family. The house was a ruin in 1392.
The rectangular wet moat east of the village centre marks the site.

LEIGH CASTLE   SO 781519

On a low lying, and probably
once marshy, site at Castle
Green, 1km WSW of Bransford,
is an overgrown motte rising
about 6m high from the bottom
of the surrounding ditch with
an outer bank to the west and
north.   The mound summit is
about 20m in diameter. To the
south is a round bailey plat-
-form about 3m high and 40m
across.

Henry III took the castle
of Leigh, probably founded in
the 12th century, from Hugh
de Pembridge, a noted rebel,
and gave it to Matthew de
Gamages. Shortly after Hugh
de Pembridge's death in 1272
his son recovered the lands,
which were held from Pershore
Abbey.

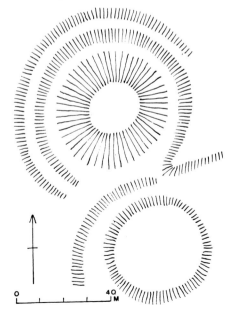

PLAN OF LEIGH CASTLE

61

ROCHFORD MOTTE

SO 629685

Beside the River Teme north of Rochford Church is a worn down motte now about 2m high.

STRENSHAM CASTLE

SO 904405

James Russell was licensed to have an oratory at his house at Lower Strensham in 1283. He was then only a tenant but in 1298 he bought the property. In 1388 Richard II licensed his Master of Horse, Sir John Russell, to crenellate the house. Sir William Russell was made a baronet in 1627 by Charles I, and was the Royalist governor of Worcester during the Civil War. His seat at Strensham also appears to have been a royalist stronghold, and was probably destroyed by Parliament as a result. At the Restoration Sir William built a new seat at Strensham Court. It was entirely rebuilt in 1824.

Strensham Castle site.

No masonry remains standing of the medieval castle but behind Moat Farm is a platform measuring about 35m by 30m surrounded by a wet moat crossed by a causeway on the west side. About 15m away is a concentric outer moat, also still full of water except at the SW corner. The area between the two, now covered in vegetation, has a low bank with angular bastions at the corners, evidently a relic of the Civil War period.

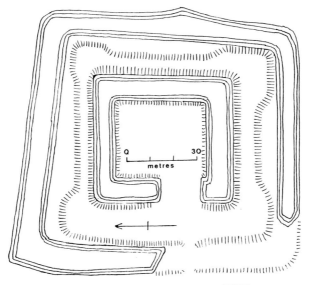

PLAN OF STRENSHAM CASTLE

WORCESTER CASTLE

SO 849547

In 1069 Ursé D'Abitot, sheriff of Worcestershire, greatly annoyed Ealdred, former Bishop of Worcester, and now Archbishop of York, by cutting off part of the cemetery of Worcester cathedral-priory for the outer defences of a newly built motte and bailey castle. The motte, which was finally removed in 1848, lay beside the river and rose 24m above it. An inner bailey lay to the east, and to the north, on the site now occupied by College Green, was the outer bailey. The Beauchamp family, as hereditary sheriffs of Worcester, held the castle throughout the 12th century. The wooden buildings were destroyed in 1113 during the first of three accidental fires to break out in the city of Worcester in the 12th century. They were soon rebuilt, probably again in wood, and the motte, tower, gateway, bridge, bailey palisade, hall, chambers, and the cellars of the King's houses within the castle are all mentioned in the sheriff's acounts during the reigns of Henry II and Richard I. However, the expenditure recorded is only modest, and probably only refers to repairs. In 1204 King John, who frequently visited the city, and was buried in Worcester Cathedral in 1216, ordered the sheriff to rebuild the wooden gatehouse in stone, which was done at a cost of £40. In the conflict between John and his barons at the end of his reign Worcester Castle was held by William Marshall the younger against the King, and was attacked by the Earl of Chester and Fawkes de Breaute.

Just after King John's death the monks of the cathedral-priory petitioned Henry III for the ground taken by Urse D'Abitot in 1069 to be returned to them. The young King agreed, and the baileys were given to the monks, whilst the motte and its tower remained in the custody of Walter de Beauchamp. By this time the castle at Elmley had become the Beauchamps' main seat, and no further interest was taken in the dismembered castle at Worcester either by the sheriff or King. When Robert Ferrers, Earl of Derby, entered and sacked the city in the Barons' cause in 1263, it was 'through the old castle' indicating that it was then untenable and disused. The Beauchamps and their successors maintained an interest in the land until it was surrendered to Henry VII by Anne, Countess of Warwick, in 1487. Leland describes the castle as "clene down" and says that "half the base courte or area of it is now within the waulle of the close of the cathedrall churche". For many years the county prison stood on the other half of the site until transferred elsewhere in 1809. A map of 1741 shows not only the motte, but the southern rampart of the former inner bailey as still existing.

WORCESTER BISHOP'S PALACE   SO 849546

The former Bishop's Palace, which became the Deanery in 1842, lies to the north of the cathedral. Externally most of it dates from the time of Bishop Hough, 1717-43, and Bishop Johnston, 1759-74, who spent over £5,000 on additions, but within it are various vaulted undercrofts of the 13th century. They probably date from the time of Bishop Giffard, who was licensed to crenellate the palace in 1271. The precinct, 2 acres in extent, was presumably surrounded by a high embattled wall with a substantial gatehouse, but the various buildings within it appear to have been of a purely domestic type. The undercrofts formed part of the Bishop's hall and chapel and it is thought that there was once a large great hall to the south. Also incorporated are some featureless 12th century walls.

WORCESTER CITY WALLS

Worcester was a Roman fortress probably established in the first century AD, and refortified later. Fresh defences were constructed in 899 against the Danes by Aethelred, Earl of Mercia. Worcester received a royal charter in 1189, and in the early 13th century Henry III allowed the townsfolk to make tolls to pay for building the stone walls which stood complete until the 18th century. Of these there now remain just several low lengths on the east side with a small round turret, but no other features of interest. A fortified gateway stood upon the 14th century bridge over the Severn replaced in 1781. There were six other gateways, namely the Water Gate near the river on the NW, the Fore Gate on the north, St Martin's Gate and Friar's Gate on the east, Sidbury gate on the SE, and Frog Gate on the south. They were destroyed in the late 18th century because their narrow archways restricted traffic flows. The last to remain was St Martin's Gate, which had two octagonal towers flanking the outer portal and three parallel gables facing the city. The Sidbury Gate had round flanking towers, the base of the northern one being uncovered in 1908. Excavations have shown that outside the walls was a flat-bottomed water-filled ditch 12m wide. Worcester was in late 1642 occupied by a Parliamentary army under the Earl of Essex but throughout most of the Civil war was a Royalist stronghold and withstood an attack by Sir William Waller in 1643. It surrendered only in July 1646. The worn down bastioned fortlet commanding the site of Sidbury Gate is a relic of the Commonwealth period.

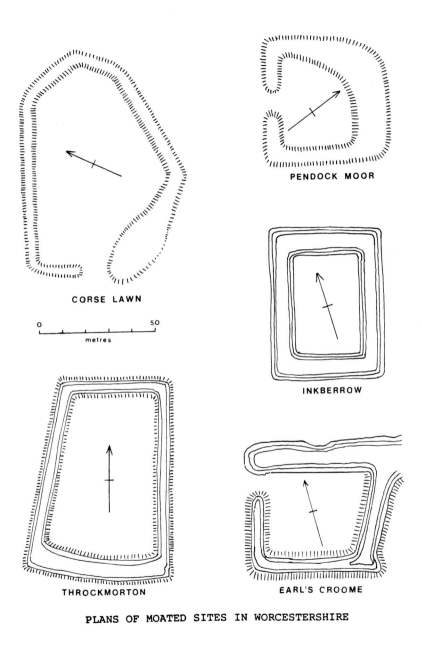

CORSE LAWN

PENDOCK MOOR

INKBERROW

THROCKMORTON

EARL'S CROOME

0   50

metres

PLANS OF MOATED SITES IN WORCESTERSHIRE

LIST OF MOATED SITES IN WORCESTERSHIRE

ABBOTS MORTON SP 026551 A dry moat lies by a house in the village.
ASTWOOD COURT SP 032623 An oval wet moat surrounds the house.
BANNALS FARM SO 644637 A fragment of a moat lies beside the house.
BENTLEY SO 989664 A rectangular wet moat lies in a field.
BIRTSMORTON COURT SO 801355 House is surrounded by a wet moat.
BLACKGREVES SP 066755 A rectangular moat surrounds the farmhouse.
BOWERCOURT SO 736707 Part of a wet moat lies by the farm.
CHURCHILL SO 923536 Part of a moat lies near the church.
CORSE LAWN SO 824304 A wedge-shaped moat lies in fields.
COTHERIDGE SO 775557 A dry moat surrounds Moat Cottage.
CROOKBARROW HILL SO 876524 Part of a wet moat lies by a house.
CROWLE SO 922559 A dry fragment of a moat lies near the church.
DUNSTALL SO 883427 Two arms of a wet moat lie beside a house.
EARLS CROOME SO 873420 Rectangular platform in partly wet moat.
EARDISTON SO 696681 Part of a moat lies beside Moor Farm.
ELMLEY CASTLE SO 985402 Two arms of wet moat in field E of castle.
FAIRFIELD SO 946758 Deep dry moat around garden of house.
FECKENHAM SP 008615 An earthwork lies in a field by the village.
GANNOW GREEN SO 984784 A rectangular moat lies in a field.
HANLEY SWAN SO 814435 Part of a wet moat lies by a stream.
HARDWICK GREEN SO 817327 Three sides of a wet moat beside a farm.
HARVINGTON SO 877745 An irregularly shaped moat surrounds the hall.
HILL CROOME SO 885409 Part of a wet moat lies beside Manor Farm.
HOLBERROW GREEN SP 013597 Rectangular moat by house. 2nd moat nearby.
HUDDINGTON COURT SO 944573 Rectangular moat lies around the house.
HUNNINGTON SO 963812 Three sides of a moat lie in a field.
LONGDON SO 839361 Two arms of a wet moat lie beside a house.
LULSLEY SO 746555 A rectangular wet moat lies beside a house.
MADRESFIELD SO 809474 Three sides of a wet moat surround the house.
MOON'S MOAT SP 069682 Three sides of a wet moat lie in a field.
MOORGREEN HALL SP 054743 A dry rectangular moat lies in a field.
MORTON UNDERHILL SP 013591 Just a pool remains by a house.
NAUNTON BEAUCHAMP SO 959523 A dry moat lies in a field.
NORTON SO 872515 Two arms of a wet moat remain near the barracks.
PENDOCK MOOR SO 814348 A dry rectangular moat lies in a field.
PIGEON HOUSE FARM SO 810312 Two arms of a wet moat beside a farm.
PRIORY FARM SP 053573 An oval wet moat lies by the farm.
ROCHFORD SO 634673 Rectangular moat.
ROCK SO 733710 A partly wet moat lies south of the church.
ROUS LENCH SP 016533 Rectangular dry moat in field by church.
SHERRARDS GREEN SO 798462 Rectangular wet moat around farm.
SHURNOCK SP 027608 Part of circular wet moat around farm.
SODINGTON HALL SO 693709 A fragment of a moat lies by the farm.
STOCK WOOD SP 003591 Three arms of a moat remain by the house.
SUCKLEY COURT SO 714514 Fragments of a wet moat lie beside farm.
TANNERS GREEN SP 088744 Fragments of a moat lie in fields.
THE ELMS SO 796574 An oval wet moat lies in fields.
THROCKMORTON SO 982499 Square wet moat by church. Other moats nearby.
TOOKEYS FARM SP 040618 Part of a wet moat remains by a house.
WARNDON SO 888577 House beside church still has a moat.
WHITE LADIES ASTON SO 925521 Three sides of a wet moat by house.
WOODEND FARM SO 777574 Two arms of a wet moat lie beside farm.
WOODMANTON FARM SO 718605 A fragment of a moat lies by the farm.

Note: Water levels in moats can vary quite considerably.

For a longer list of moats see the Victoria County History IV p427.

MAP OF CASTLES IN WORCESTERSHIRE

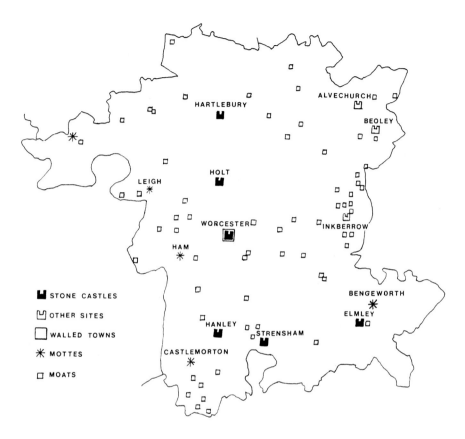

BIBLIOGRAPHY

The Buildings of Herefordshire, Nikolaus Pevsner, 1963
The Buildings of Worcestershire, Nikolaus Pevsner, 1968
Victoria County History of Herefordshire
Victoria County History of Worcestershire (4 vols)
Royal Commission on Historical Monuments Inventory for Herefordshire
A History of The Castles of Herefordshire, C.Robinson, 1869
A History of The Mansions & Manors of Herefordshire, C.Robinson, 1873
Herefordshire Under Arms, Charles Hopkinson, 1985
A History of Herefordshire, John & Margaret West, 1985
Transactions of the Woolhope Naturalists' Field Club
Norman Castles in Britain, Derek Renn, 1968.
Hanley Castle....Heart of Malvern Chase, Pamela Hurle, 1978

GLOSSARY OF TERMS

Apse   - Semi-circular or polygonal shaped structure.
Ashlar   - Masonry of blocks with even faces and square edges.
Barbican   - Porch, tower, or enclosure defending a gateway.
Bastion   - Flanking projection of same height as the main wall.
Batter   - The inward inclination of a wall face.
Battlement   - A parapet with crenellations protecting a wallwalk.
Chevrons   - A series of Vs forming a zig-zag pattern.
Crenellations   - Indentations in a parapet.
Curtain Walls   - High stone walls around a castle bailey.
Forebuilding   - A fortified porch defending the entrance of a keep.
Garderobe   - A latrine or small changing room.
Hall Keep   - A rectangular keep which is longer than it is high.
Hoarding   - Wooden gallery at a wall top providing macholations.
Jamb   - The side of a doorway, window, or other opening.
Keep   - A building or a small court acting as a citadel.
Light   - A compartment of a window.
Machicolation   - A slot for dropping or firing missiles.
Merlons   - The upstanding portions of a crenellated parapet.
Moat   - A ditch, wet or dry, around an enclosure.
Motte   - Steep mound, usually at least partly artificial.
Mullion   - A vertical member dividing the lights of a window.
Parapet   - A wall for protection at any sudden drop.
Piscina   - Stone basin for rinsing out holy vessels after mass.
Portcullis   - Gate designed to rise and fall in vertical grooves.
Postern   - A secondary gateway or back doorway.
Ringwork   - A small enclosure with a high rampart around it.
Roll Moulding   - Moulding of semi-circular or D-shaped section.
Screens   - Service end of a hall, usually screened off.
Shell Keep   - Small stone walled enclosure on top of a motte.
Solar   - Castle owner's living room, often also his bedroom.
Transom   - Horizontal member dividing top & bottom window lights.
Turning Bridge - A bridge turning vertically about a central pivot.
Wall Walk   - A walkway on a wall top, protected by a parapet.